Aardman presents

Wallace & Gromit ™

A Pier Too Far

Titan Books

Wallace & Gromit™
A Pier Too Far

HB ISBN 1 84023 953 0
PB ISBN 1 84023 958 1

Published by Titan Books,
a division of Titan Publishing Group Ltd.
144 Southwark Street
London SE1 0UP
In association with Aardman Animation Ltd.

Grateful thanks and salutations to Dick Hansom and Rachael Carpenter
at Aardman Animations, and David Barraclough, Emily Norris, Bob
Kelly, Angie Thomas, Jamie Boardman and Katy Wild at Titan Books.

A CIP catalogue record for this title is available at the British Library.

Hardback edition: September 2005
Paperback edition: March 2006

1 3 5 7 9 10 8 6 4 2

Printed in Italy.

What did you think of this book? We love to
hear from our readers. Please email us at:
readerfeedback@titanemail.com, or write to us
at the above address.

www.titanbooks.com

Aardman
presents

Wallace & Gromit™
A Pier Too Far

Original story by Simon Furman and Dan Abnett

Written by Dan Abnett

Drawn by Jimmy Hansen

Coloured by John Burns

Lettered by Richard Starkings

Edited by Simon Furman & Nick Jones

Wallace and Gromit created by Nick Park

END OF THE

STARRING...

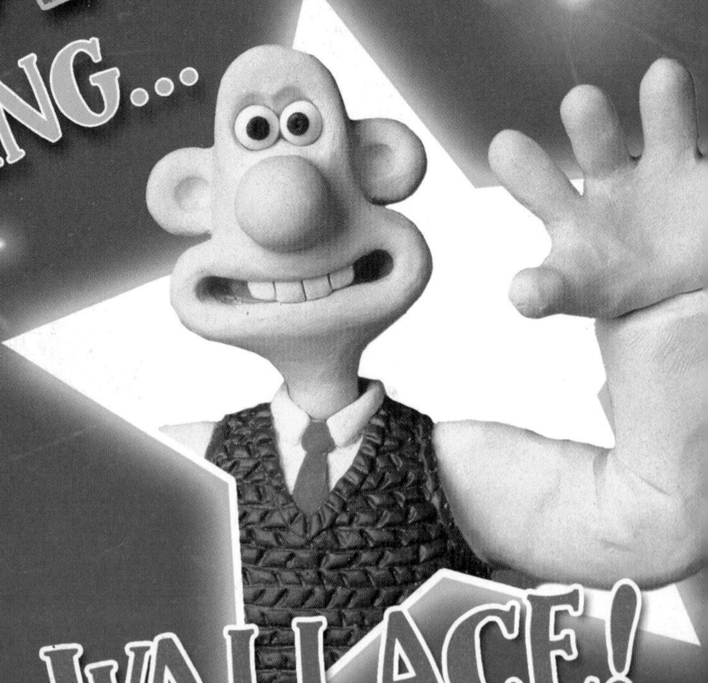

WALLACE!

Will ASTOUND you with
his improvisation!

CONFOUND you with
his inventions!

DUMBFOUND you with
his ineptness.

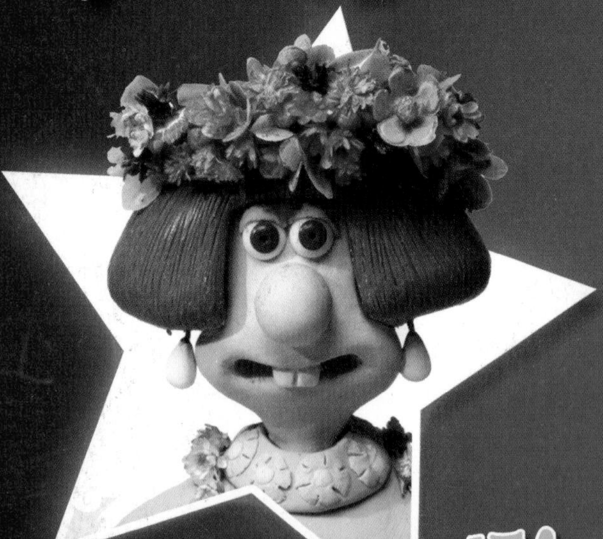

WENDOLENE!

Will SURPRISE with
her supportiveness!

TURN YOUR HEAD with
her twin set!

WOW you with
her wooliness!

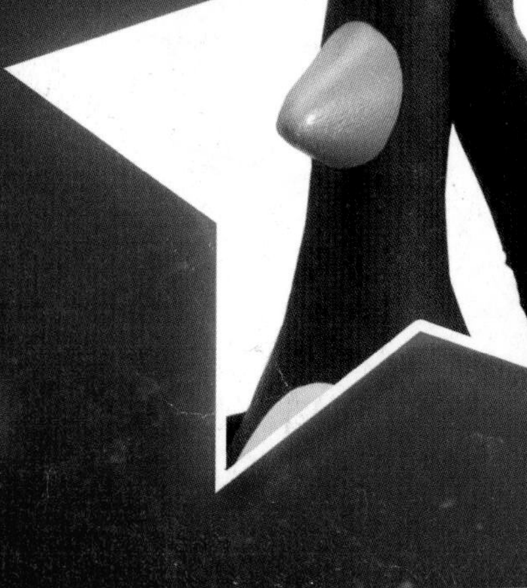

FEATHERS McGRAW!

Will SPELLBIND you with
his sparklers!

ENTICE with his ice!

Strike DUMB with his stretch!

IER SPECIAL!

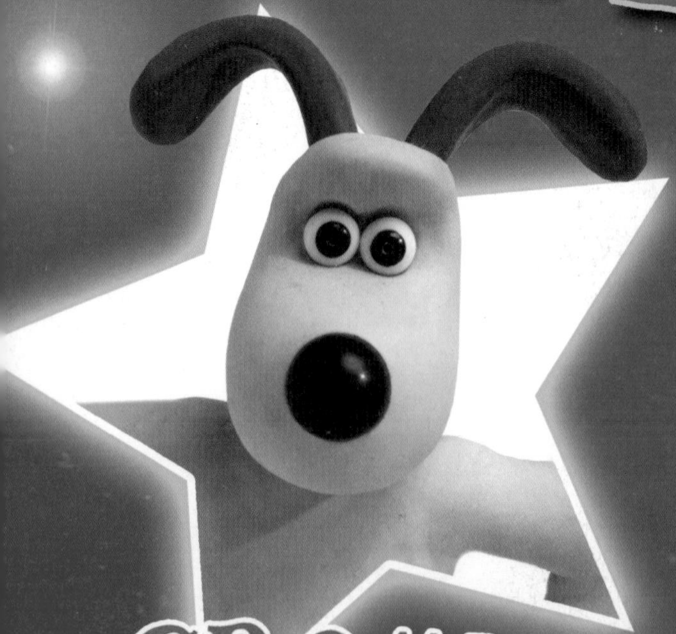

GROMIT!

Will AMAZE you with his acrobatics!

DAZZLE you with his derring-do!

TANTALISE you with his tango!

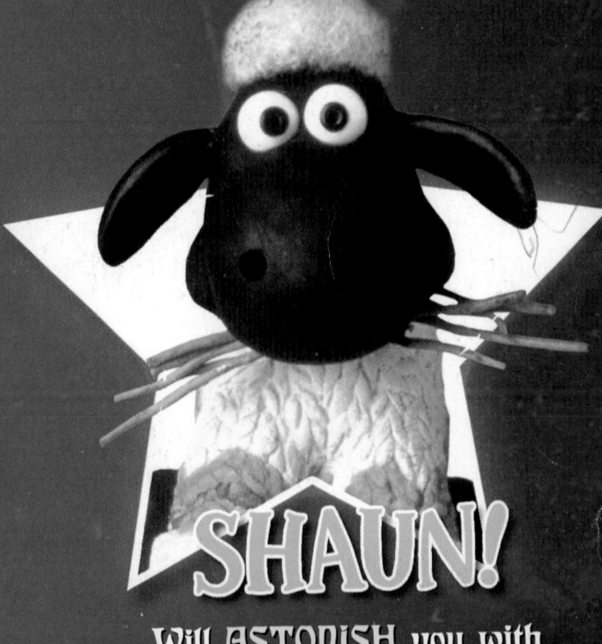

SHAUN!

Will ASTONISH you with his appetite!

STAGGER you with his swagger!

BEGGAR you with his barefaced cheek!

PRESTON!

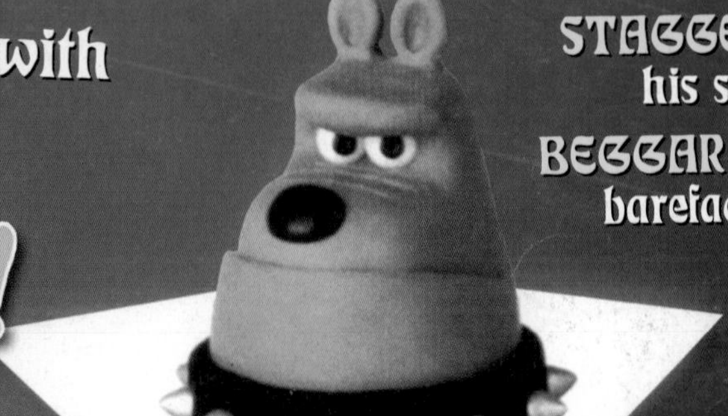

Will ELECTRIFY you with his electronics!

Create FASCINATION with his machinations!

Make an IMPRESSION with his compression!

PRESTON MARK

Dear Wendolene,

Having a cracking time!
Wish you were here...
TO FILL UP SOME EMPTY DECKCHAIRS!
Talent show going well...
WITHOUT ME!
Please remember to feed Shaun...
OR HE'LL EAT MY KNITTING!

See you soon,
Wallace AND GROMIT!

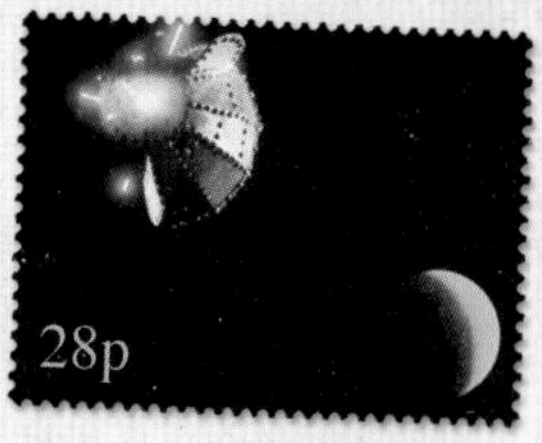

28p

Wendolene
The Wool Shop
Nr. West Wallaby Street

imsa
5-6 season
rpe fc (a)
Rovers (h)
h United (a)

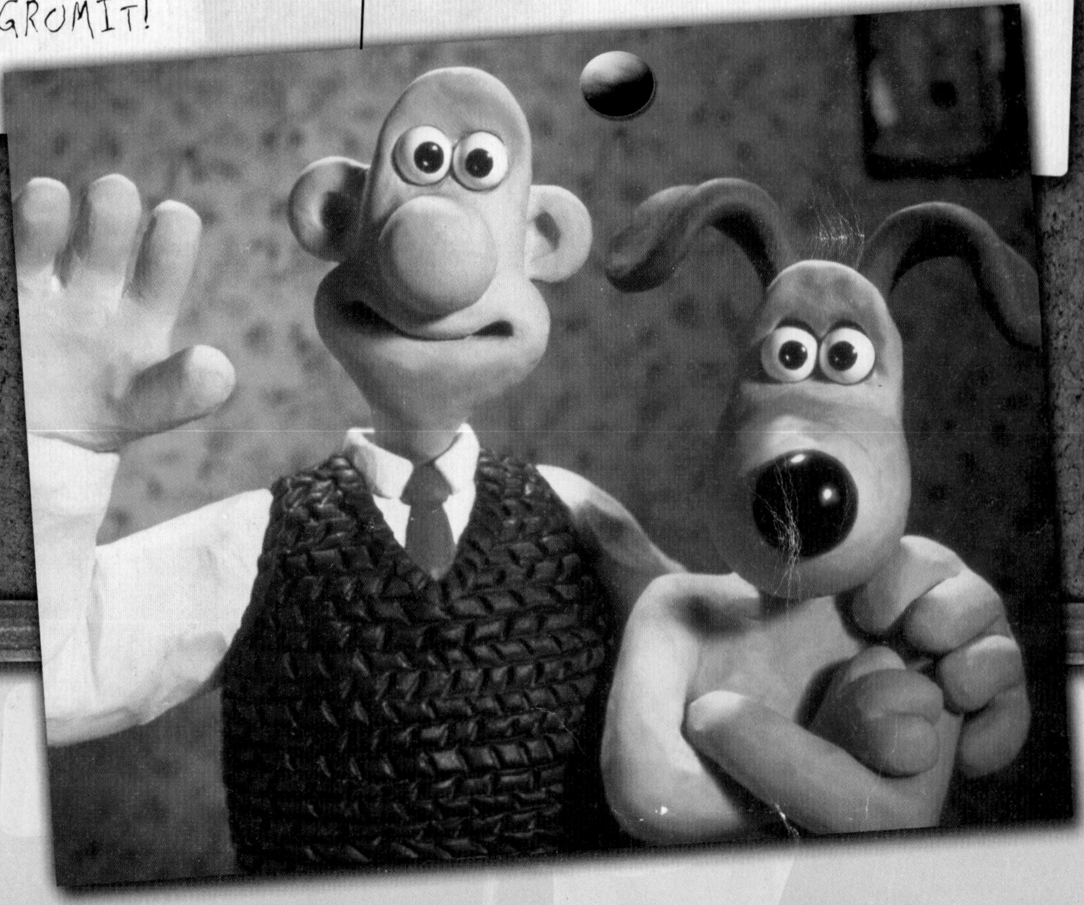

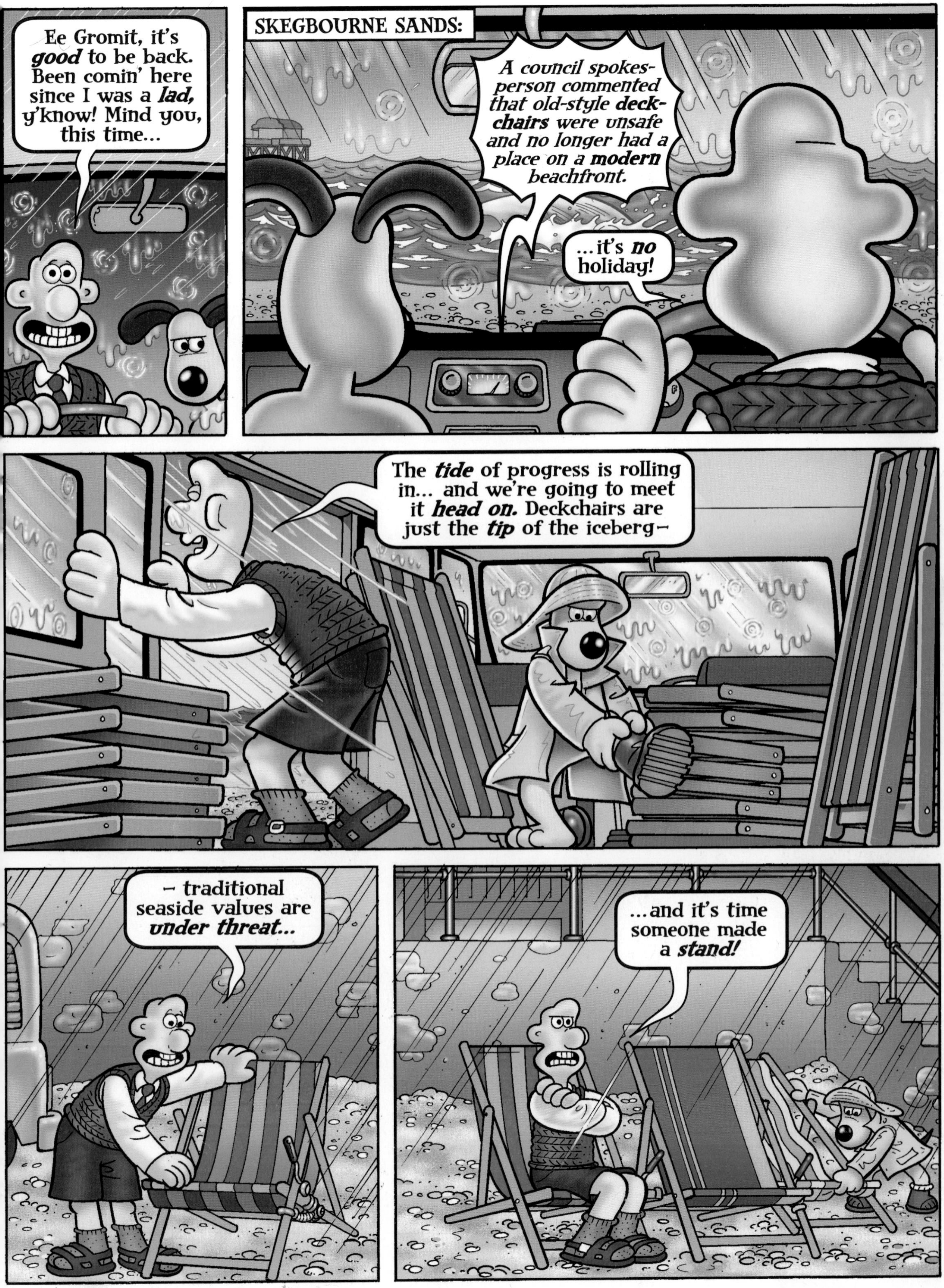
Ee Gromit, it's *good* to be back. Been comin' here since I was a *lad,* y'know! Mind you, this time...
SKEGBOURNE SANDS:
A council spokes-person commented that old-style **deck-chairs** were unsafe and no longer had a place on a **modern** beachfront.
...it's ***no*** holiday!
The ***tide*** of progress is rolling in... and we're going to meet it ***head on.*** Deckchairs are just the ***tip*** of the iceberg–
– traditional seaside values are ***under threat...***
...and it's time someone made a ***stand!***

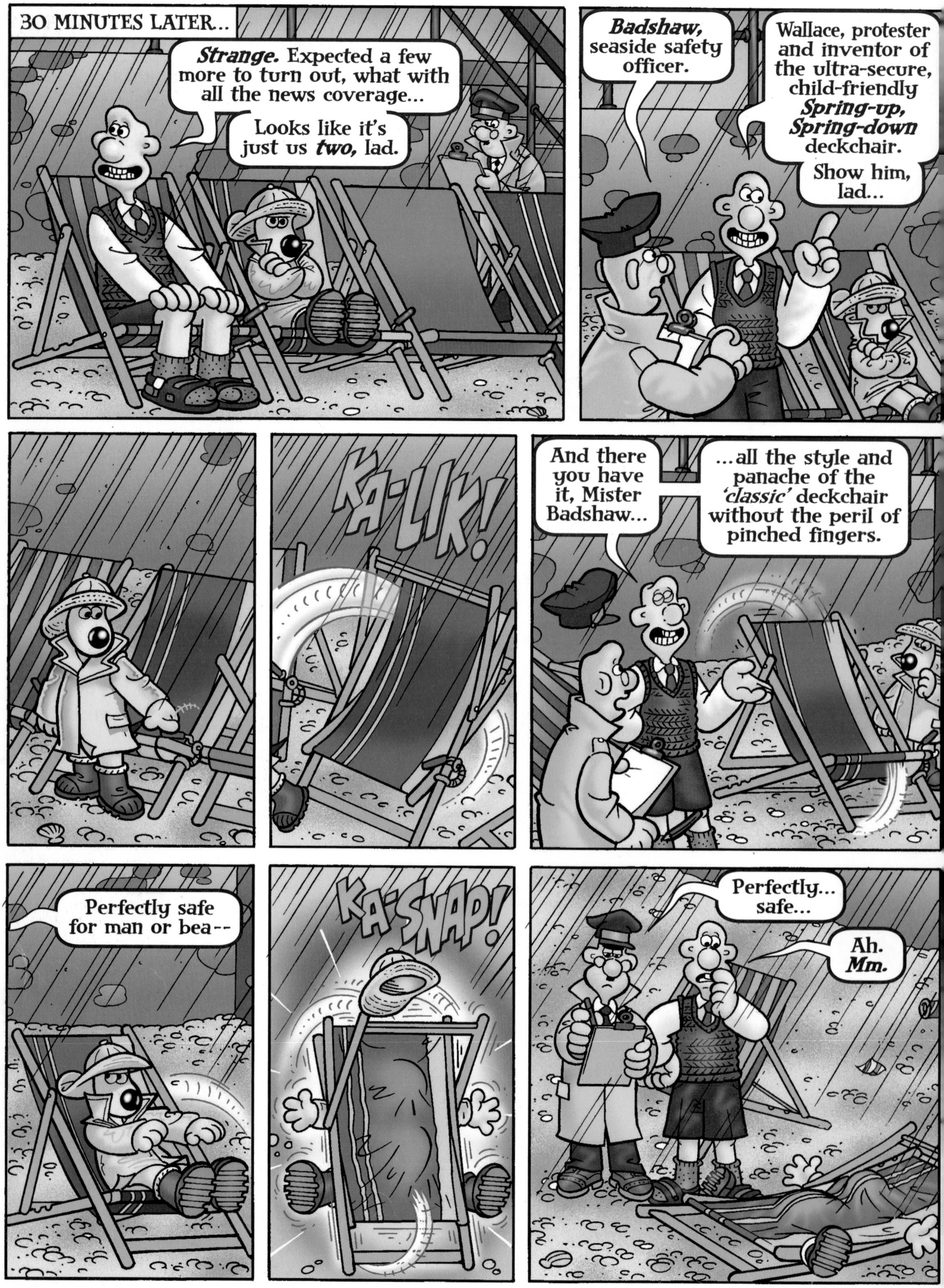

30 MINUTES LATER...
Strange. Expected a few more to turn out, what with all the news coverage...
Looks like it's just us *two,* lad.
Badshaw, seaside safety officer.
Wallace, protester and inventor of the ultra-secure, child-friendly *Spring-up, Spring-down* deckchair.
Show him, lad...
KA-LIK!
And there you have it, Mister Badshaw...
...all the style and panache of the *'classic'* deckchair without the peril of pinched fingers.
Perfectly safe for man or bea--
KA-SNAP!
Perfectly... safe...
Ah. *Mm.*

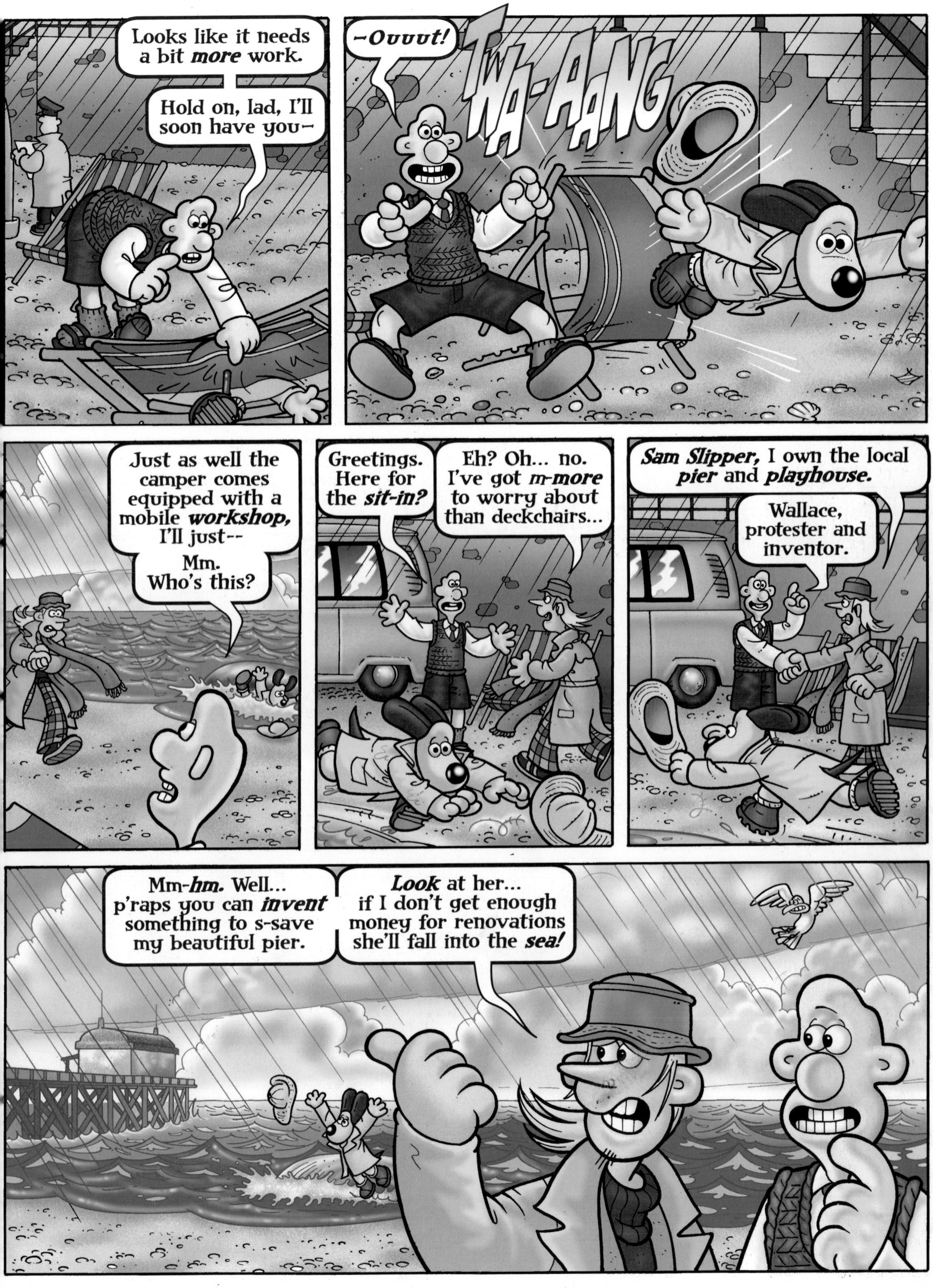
Looks like it needs a bit *more* work.
Hold on, lad, I'll soon have you—
—Ouuut!
TWA-AANG
Just as well the camper comes equipped with a mobile *workshop,* I'll just--
Mm. Who's this?
Greetings. Here for the *sit-in?*
Eh? Oh... no. I've got *m-more* to worry about than deckchairs...
Sam Slipper, I own the local *pier* and *playhouse.*
Wallace, protester and inventor.
Mm-*hm.* Well... p'raps you can *invent* something to s-save my beautiful pier.
Look at her... if I don't get enough money for renovations she'll fall into the *sea!*

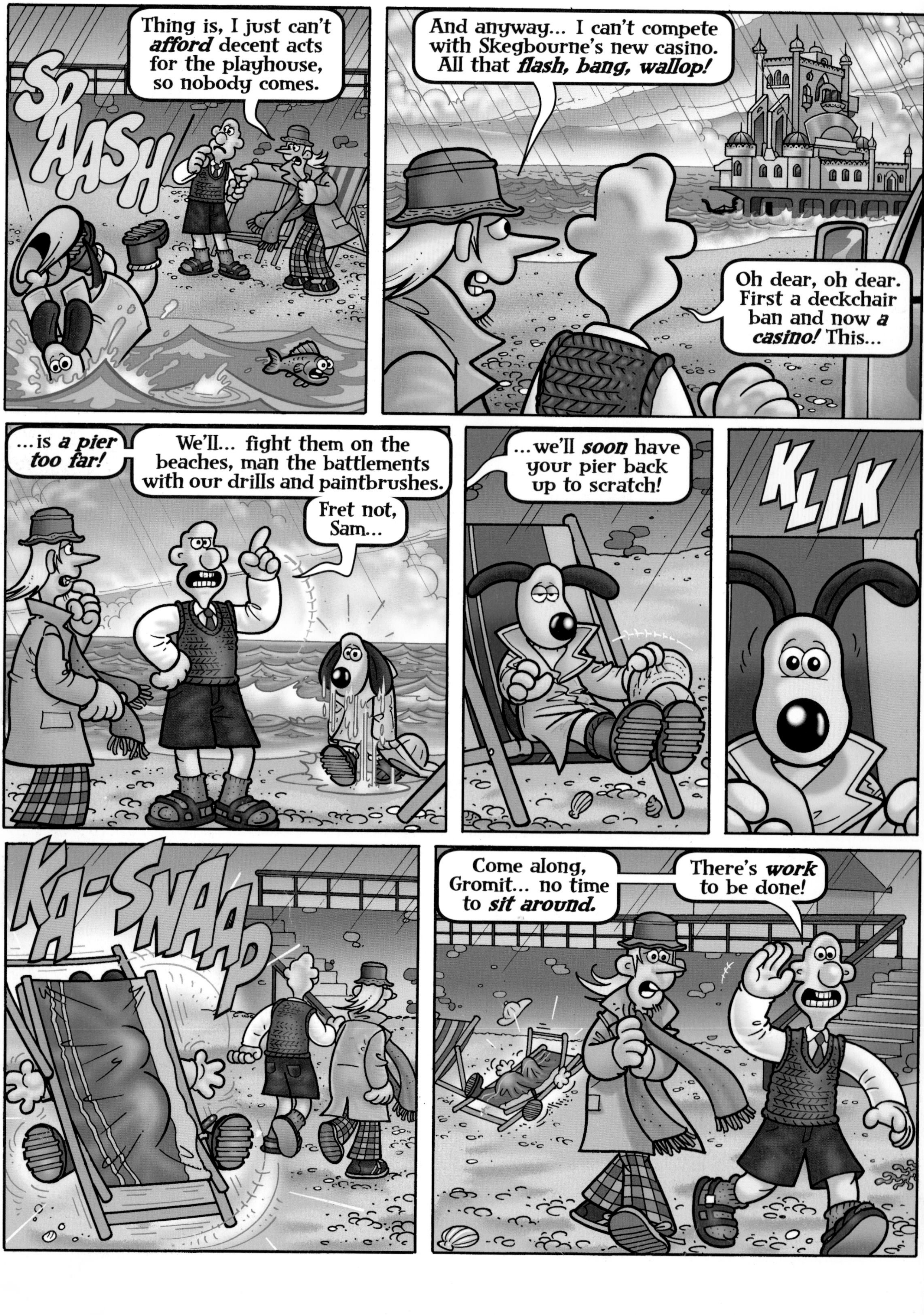
SPAASH
Thing is, I just can't *afford* decent acts for the playhouse, so nobody comes.
And anyway... I can't compete with Skegbourne's new casino. All that *flash, bang, wallop!*
Oh dear, oh dear. First a deckchair ban and now *a casino!* This...
...is *a pier too far!*
We'll... fight them on the beaches, man the battlements with our drills and paintbrushes.
Fret not, Sam...
...we'll *soon* have your pier back up to scratch!
KLIK
KA-SNAAP
Come along, Gromit... no time to *sit around.*
There's *work* to be done!

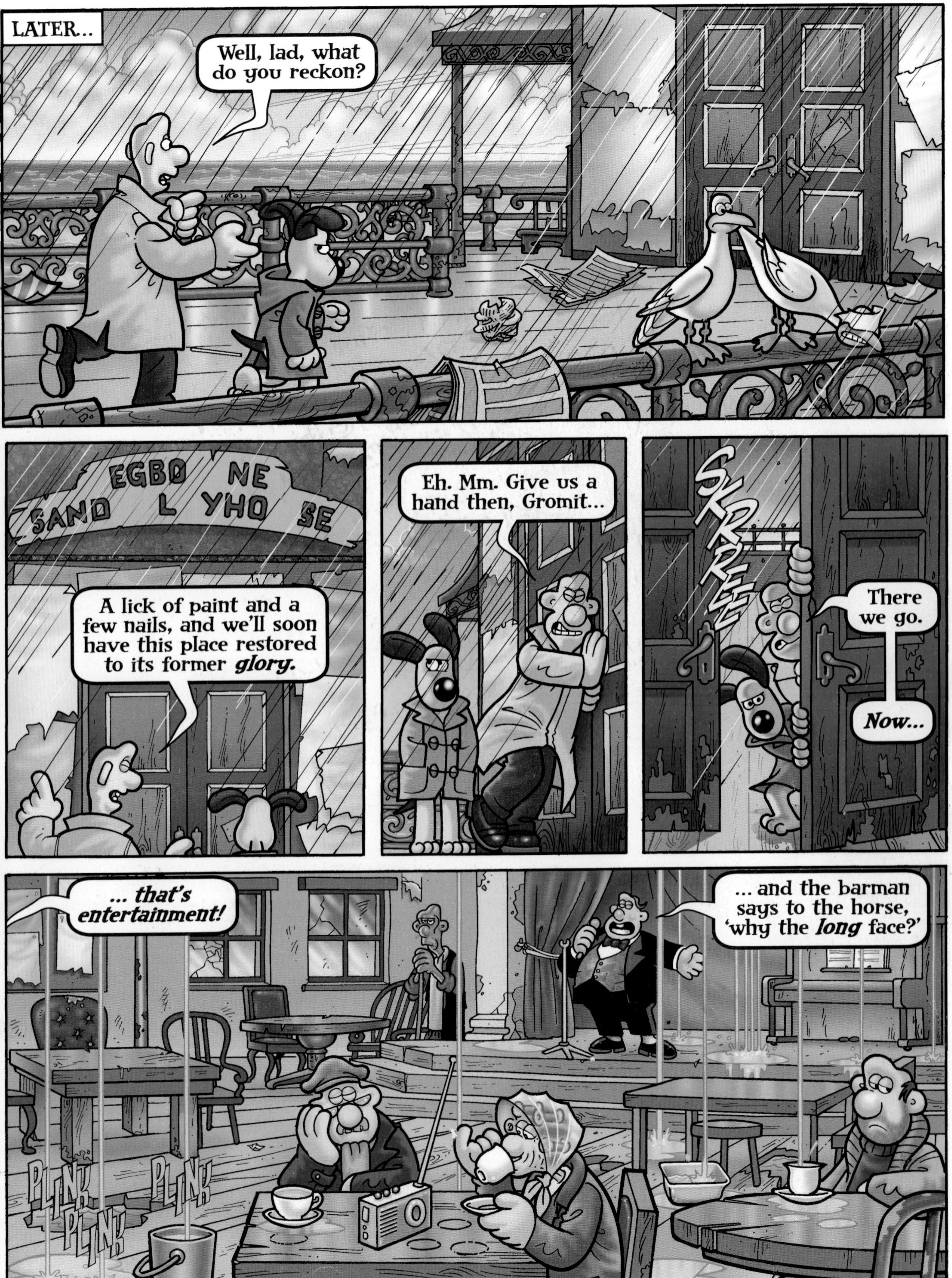
LATER...
Well, lad, what do you reckon?
EGBO NE
SAND L YHO SE
A lick of paint and a few nails, and we'll soon have this place restored to its former *glory.*
Eh. Mm. Give us a hand then, Gromit...
SKREEE
There we go.
Now...
... that's entertainment!
... and the barman says to the horse, 'why the *long* face?'
PLINK
PLINK
PLINK

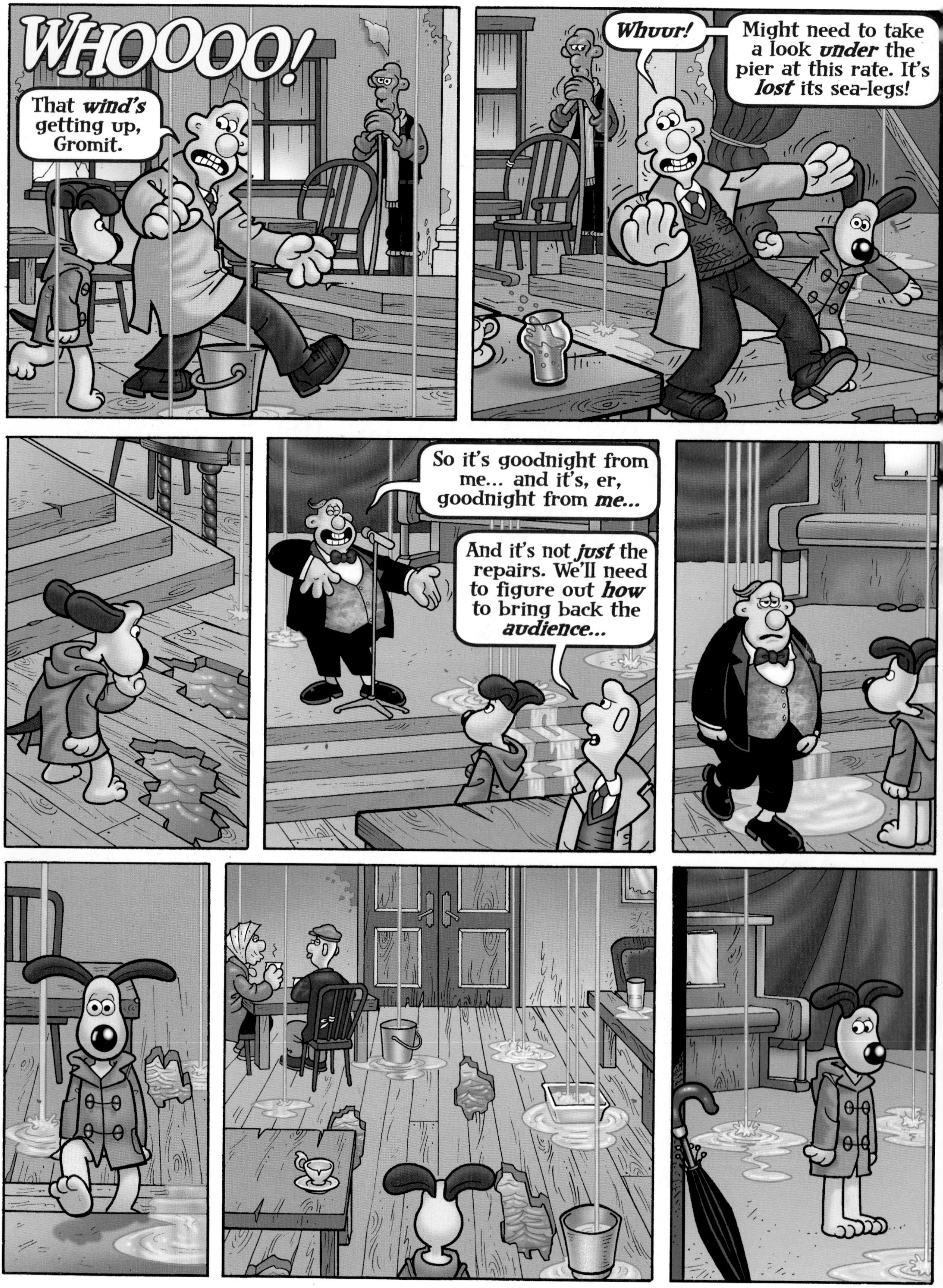
WHOOOO!
That wind's getting up, Gromit.
Whuur!
Might need to take a look under the pier at this rate. It's lost its sea-legs!
So it's goodnight from me... and it's, er, goodnight from me...
And it's not just the repairs. We'll need to figure out how to bring back the audience...

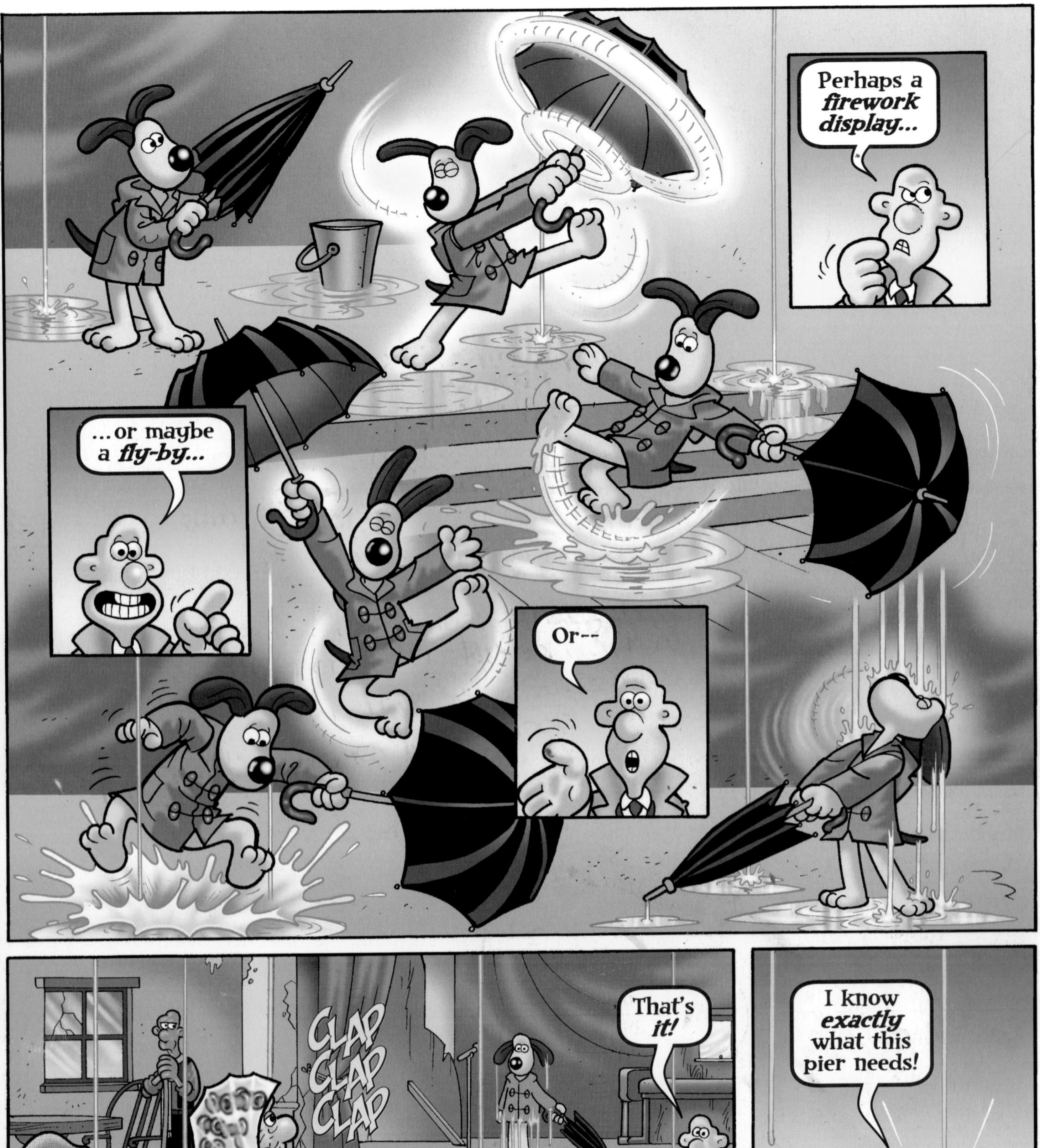
Perhaps a *firework display...*
...or maybe a *fly-by...*
Or--

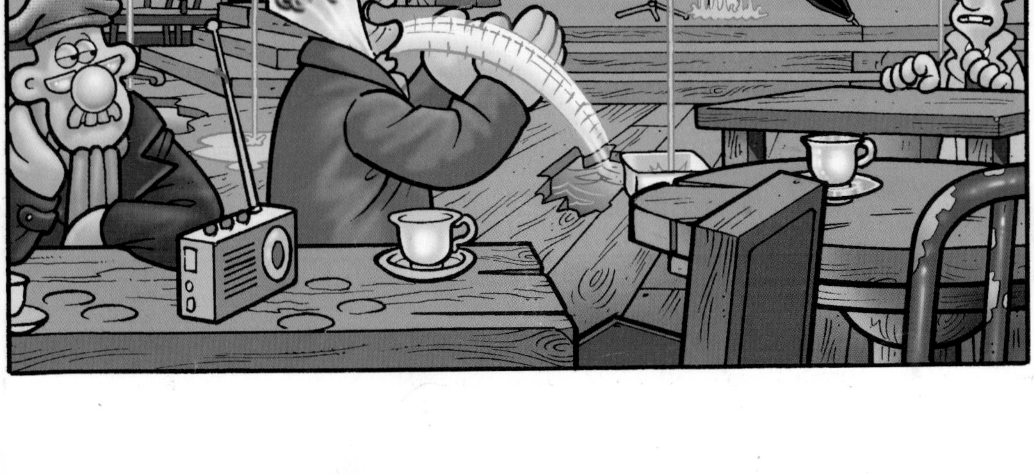
CLAP CLAP CLAP
That's *it!*

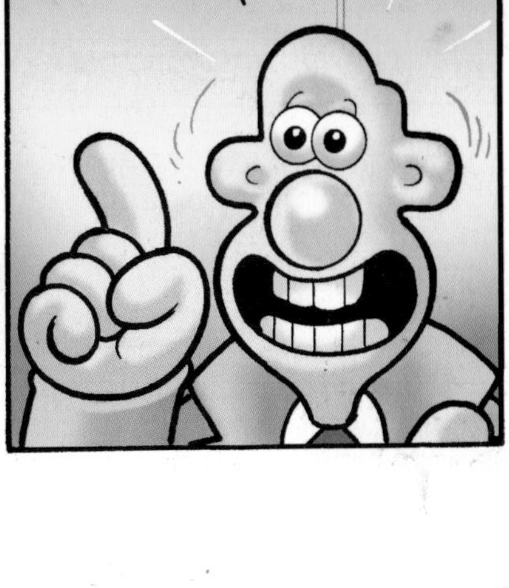
I know *exactly* what this pier needs!

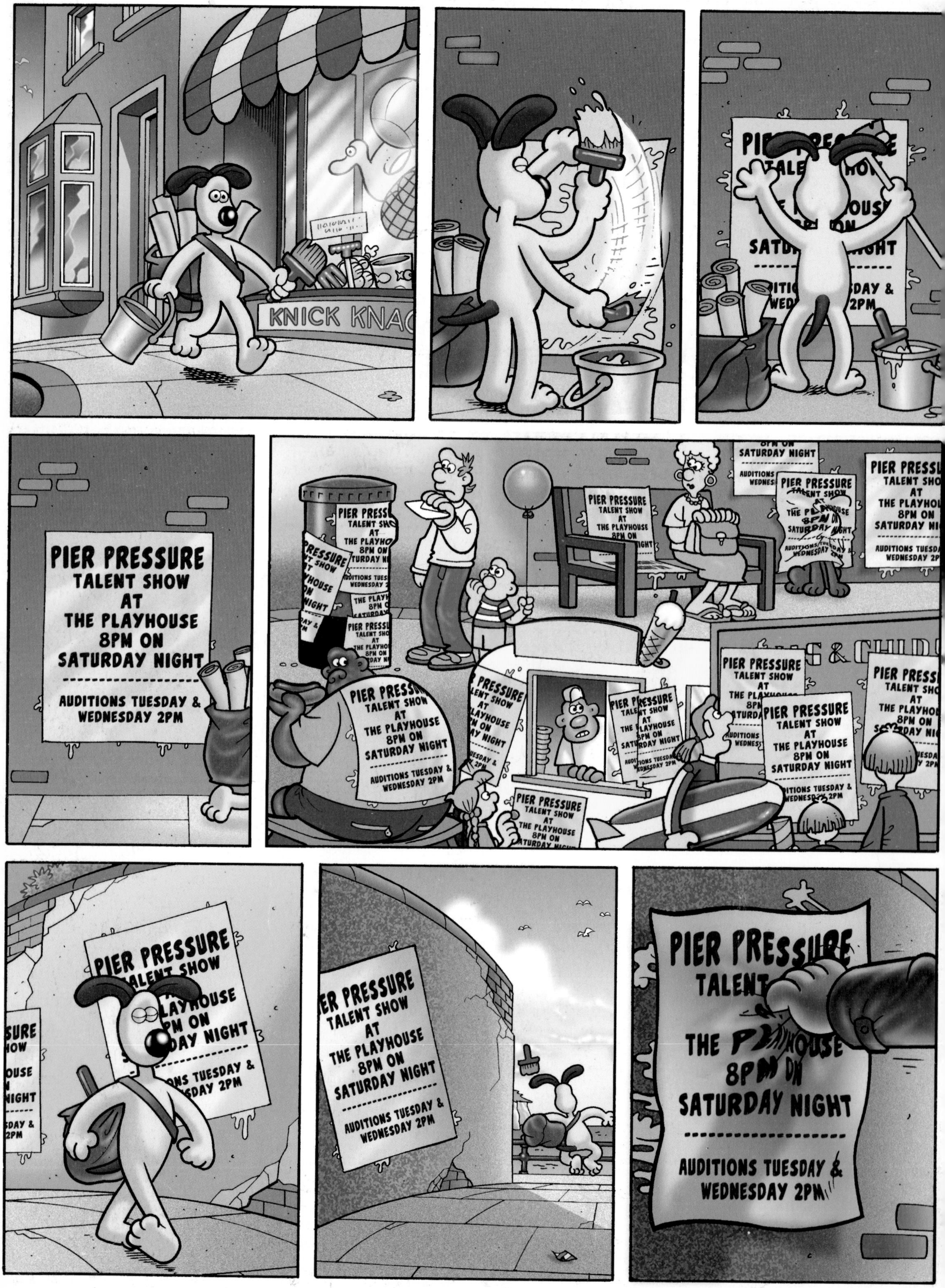
KNICK KNAC
PIER PRESSURE
TALENT SHOW
AT
THE PLAYHOUSE
8PM ON
SATURDAY NIGHT
AUDITIONS TUESDAY &
WEDNESDAY 2PM
PIER PRESSURE
TALENT SHOW
AT
THE PLAYHOUSE
8PM ON
SATURDAY NIGHT
AUDITIONS TUESDAY &
WEDNESDAY 2PM
PIER PRESSURE
TALENT SHOW
AT
THE PLAYHOUSE
8PM ON
SATURDAY NIGHT
AUDITIONS TUESDAY &
WEDNESDAY 2PM
PIER PRESSURE
TALENT
THE PLAYHOUSE
8PM ON
SATURDAY NIGHT
AUDITIONS TUESDAY &
WEDNESDAY 2PM

LATER...

What... is... the... *meaning*...

... of *this!?*

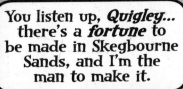

Come on, man... speak *up!* I *demand* to know who's behind such *crass* commercialism!

They're all *over* town, Mister *Burpham*, sir. I dunno--

Well *find out!* I'm the entertainment impresario round 'ere...

... and I want this fun *stopped.*

You listen up, *Quigley*... there's a *fortune* to be made in Skegbourne Sands, and I'm the man to make it.

C'mere...

... and tell me what you *see!*

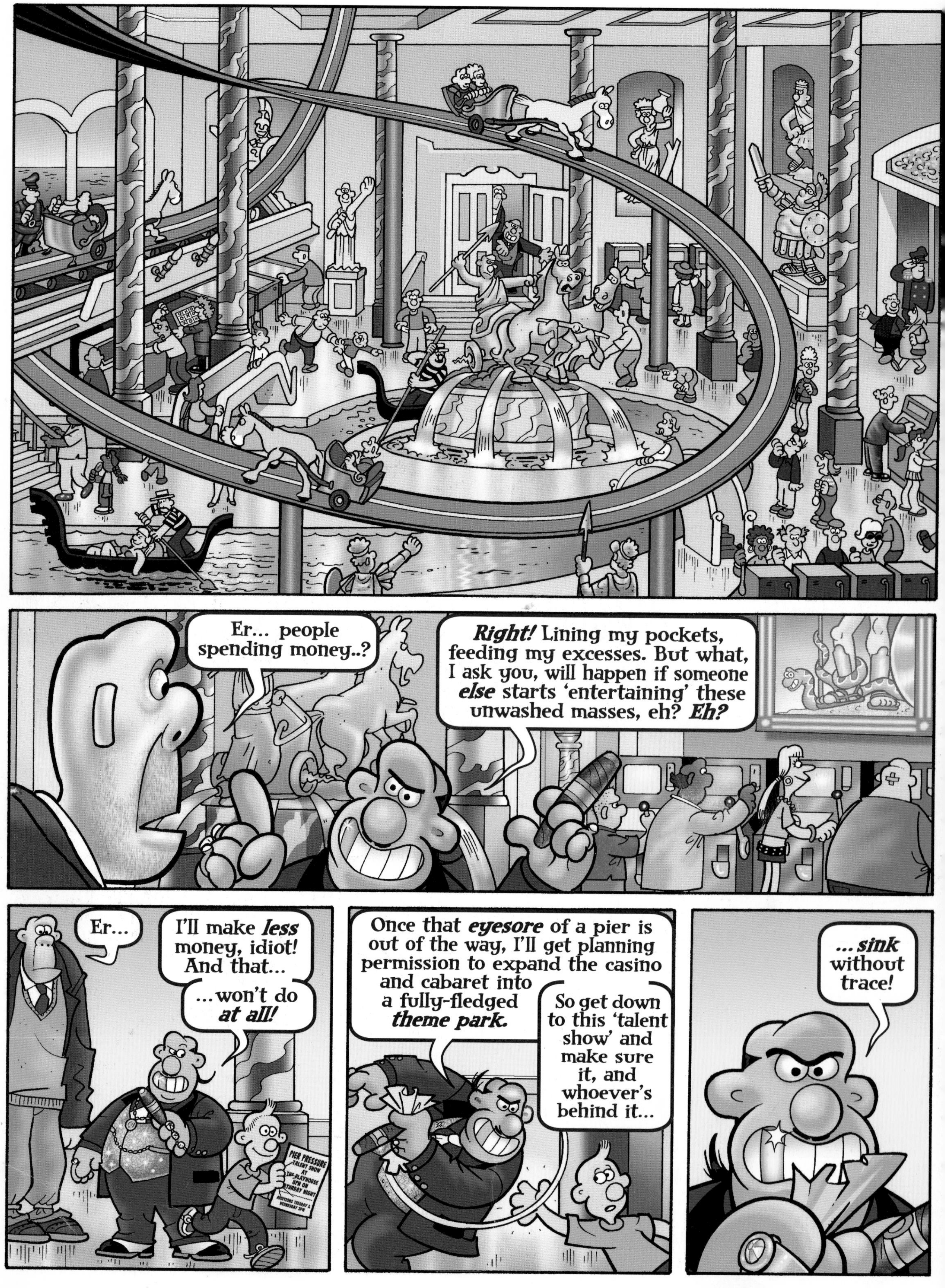
Er... people spending money..?
Right! Lining my pockets, feeding my excesses. But what, I ask you, will happen if someone *else* starts 'entertaining' these unwashed masses, eh? *Eh?*
Er...
I'll make *less* money, idiot! And that...
...won't do *at all!*
PIER PRESSURE
TALENT SHOW
Once that *eyesore* of a pier is out of the way, I'll get planning permission to expand the casino and cabaret into a fully-fledged *theme park.*
So get down to this 'talent show' and make sure it, and whoever's behind it...
...sink without trace!

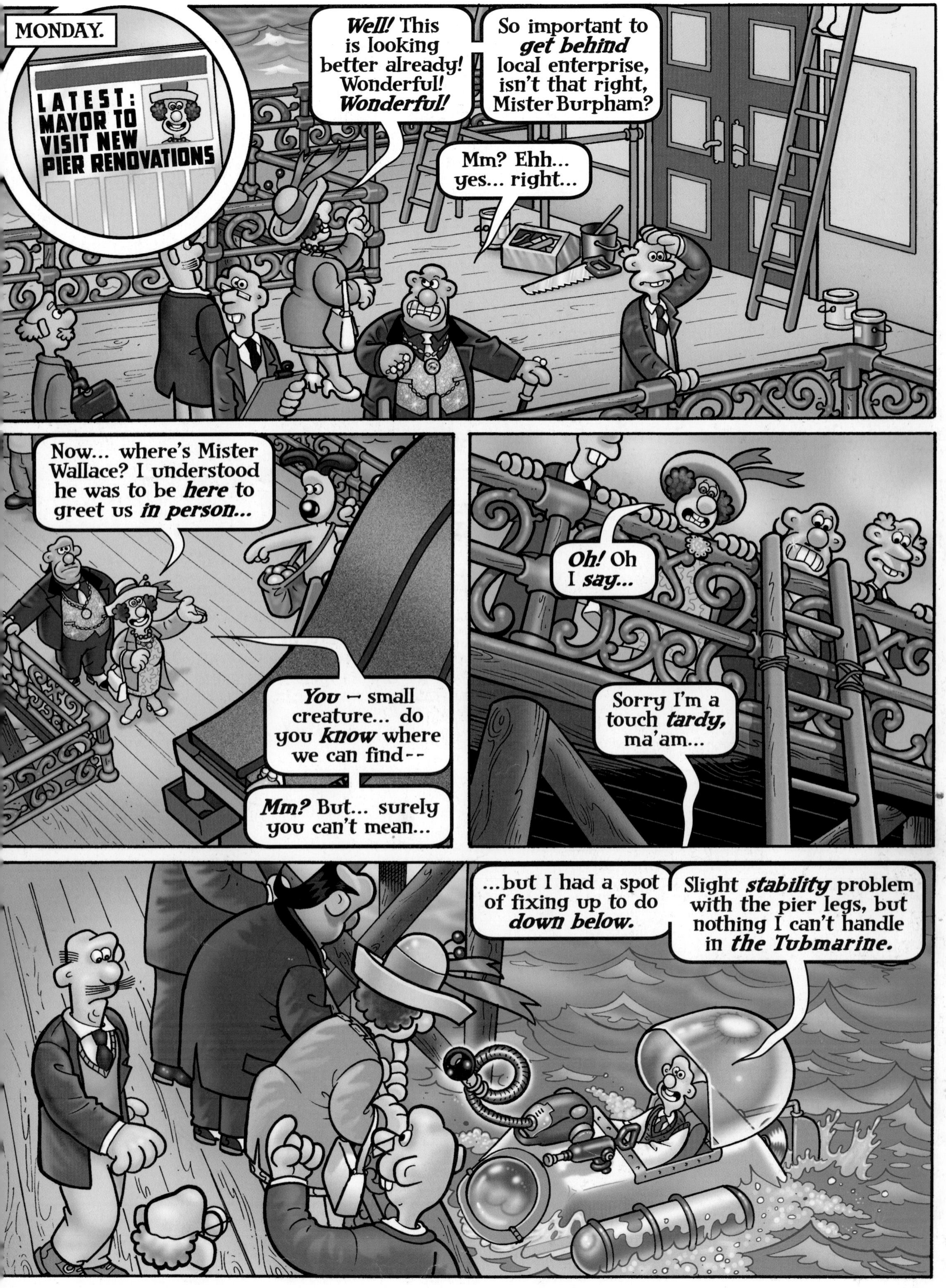

MONDAY.
LATEST: MAYOR TO VISIT NEW PIER RENOVATIONS
Well! This is looking better already! Wonderful! *Wonderful!*
So important to *get behind* local enterprise, isn't that right, Mister Burpham?
Mm? Ehh... yes... right...
Now... where's Mister Wallace? I understood he was to be *here* to greet us *in person...*
You – small creature... do you *know* where we can find--
Mm? But... surely you can't mean...
Oh! Oh I *say...*
Sorry I'm a touch *tardy,* ma'am...
...but I had a spot of fixing up to do *down below.*
Slight *stability* problem with the pier legs, but nothing I can't handle in *the Tubmarine.*

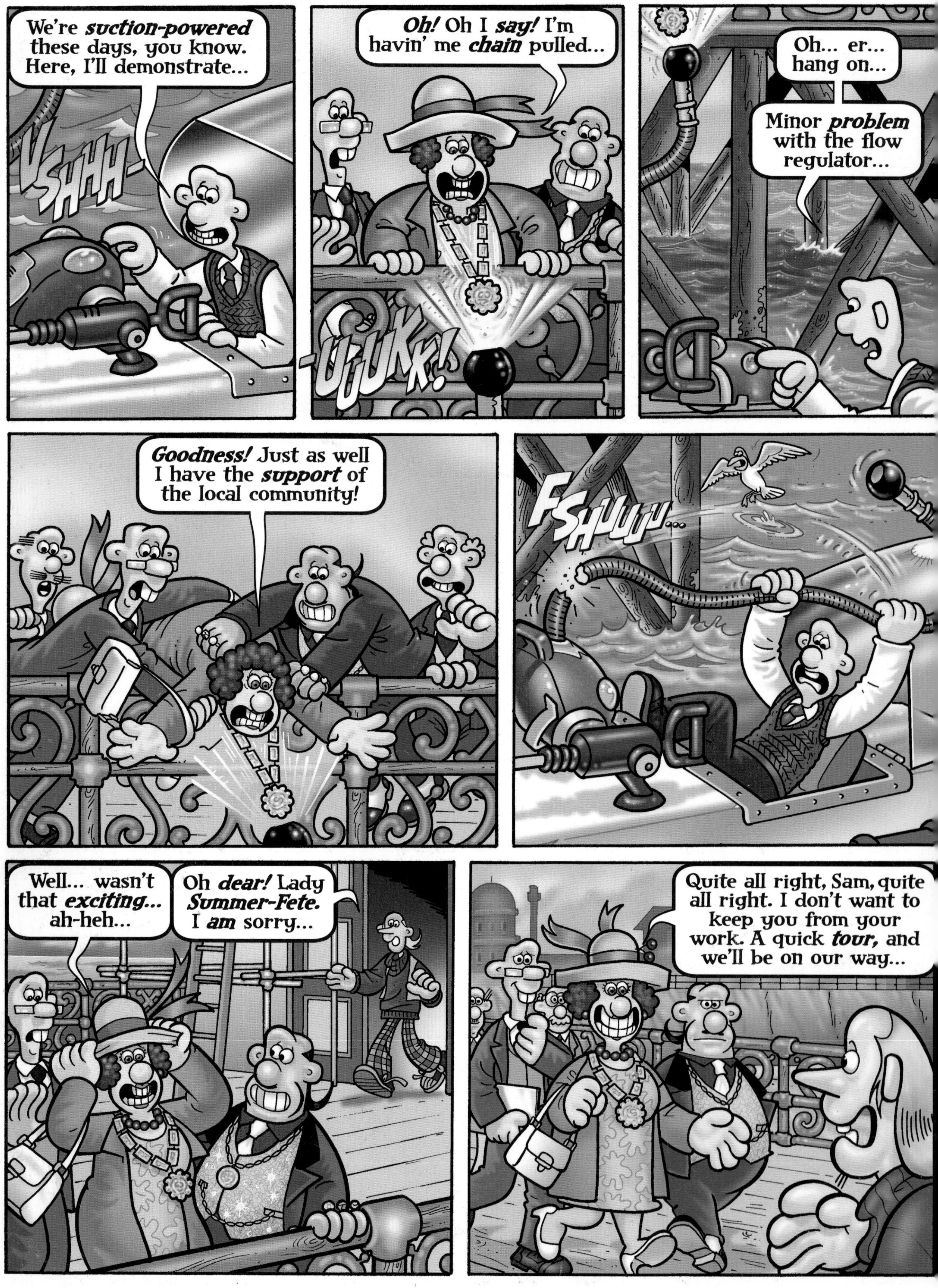
We're *suction-powered* these days, you know. Here, I'll demonstrate...
VSHHH-
Oh! Oh I *say!* I'm havin' me *chain* pulled...
-UUUKK!
Oh... er... hang on...
Minor *problem* with the flow regulator...
Goodness! Just as well I have the *support* of the local community!
FSHUUUU...
Well... wasn't that *exciting...* ah-heh...
Oh *dear!* Lady *Summer-Fete.* I *am* sorry...
Quite all right, Sam, quite all right. I don't want to keep you from your work. A quick *tour,* and we'll be on our way...

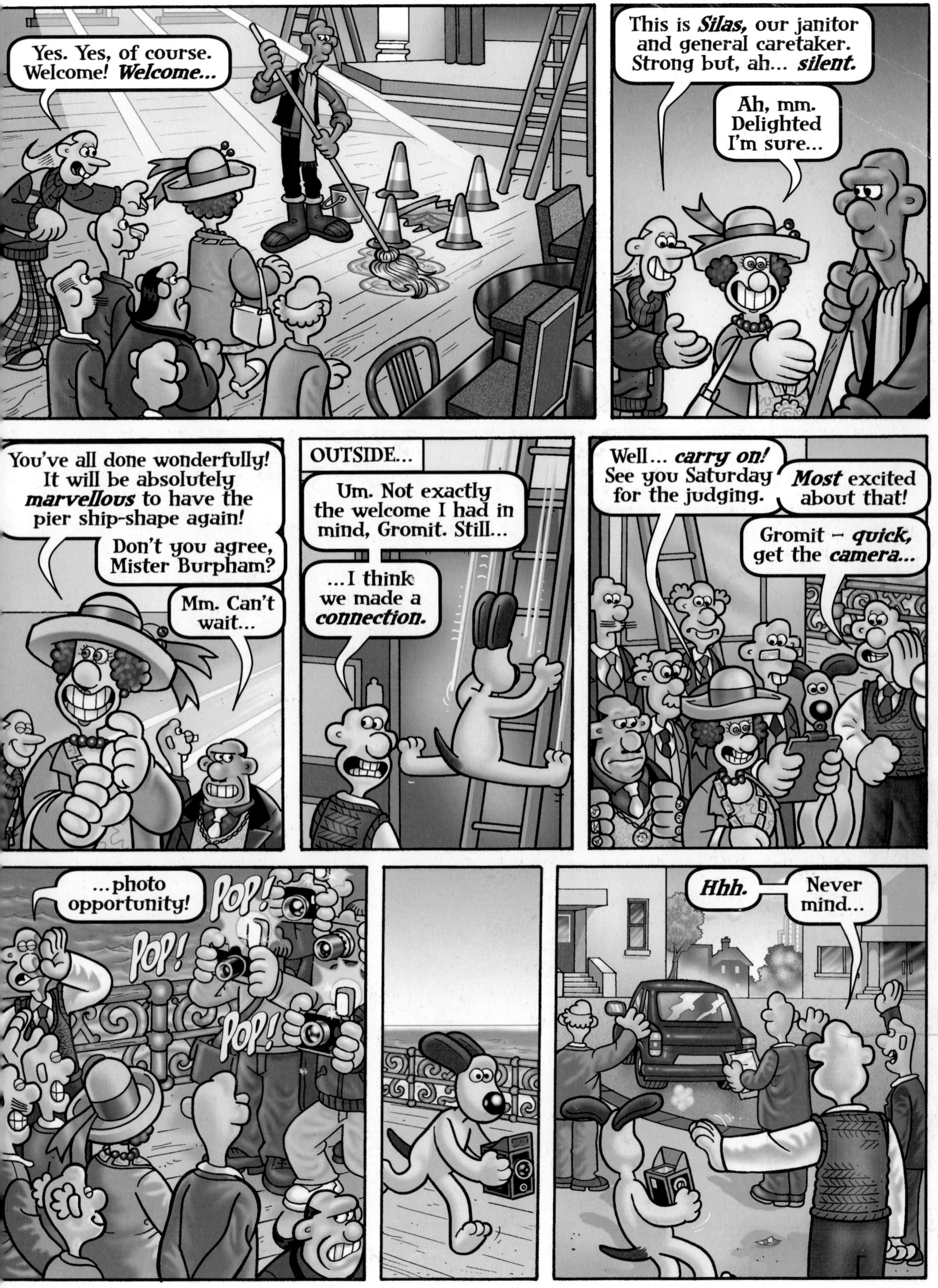

Yes. Yes, of course. Welcome! Welcome...
This is Silas, our janitor and general caretaker. Strong but, ah... silent.
Ah, mm. Delighted I'm sure...
You've all done wonderfully! It will be absolutely marvellous to have the pier ship-shape again!
Don't you agree, Mister Burpham?
Mm. Can't wait...
OUTSIDE...
Um. Not exactly the welcome I had in mind, Gromit. Still...
...I think we made a connection.
Well... carry on! See you Saturday for the judging.
Most excited about that!
Gromit – quick, get the camera...
...photo opportunity!
POP!
POP!
POP!
Hhh.
Never mind...

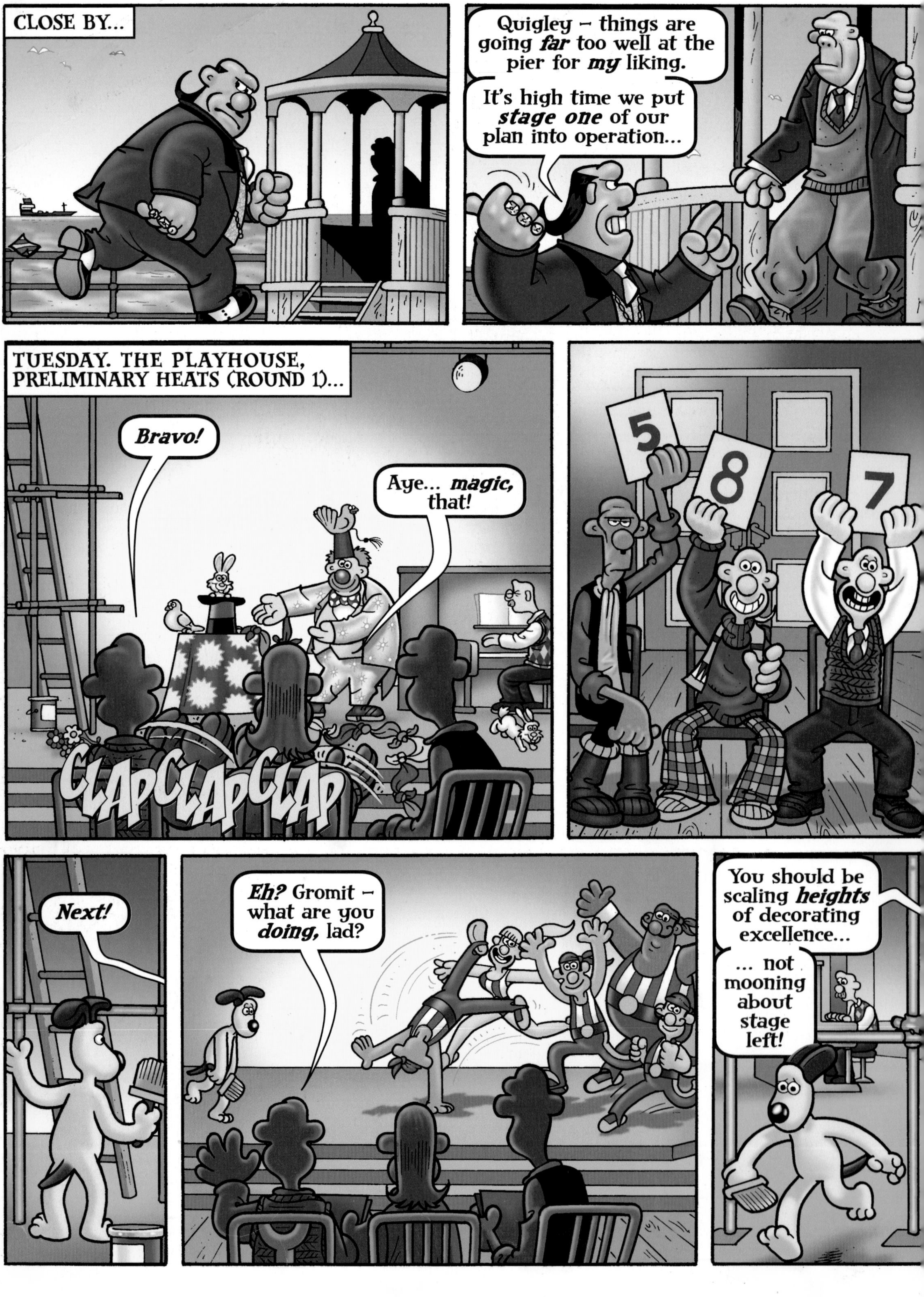

CLOSE BY...
Quigley – things are going *far* too well at the pier for *my* liking.
It's high time we put *stage one* of our plan into operation...
TUESDAY. THE PLAYHOUSE, PRELIMINARY HEATS (ROUND 1)...
Bravo!
Aye... *magic,* that!
CLAPCLAPCLAP
5
8
7
Next!
Eh? Gromit – what are you *doing,* lad?
You should be scaling *heights* of decorating excellence...
... not mooning about stage left!

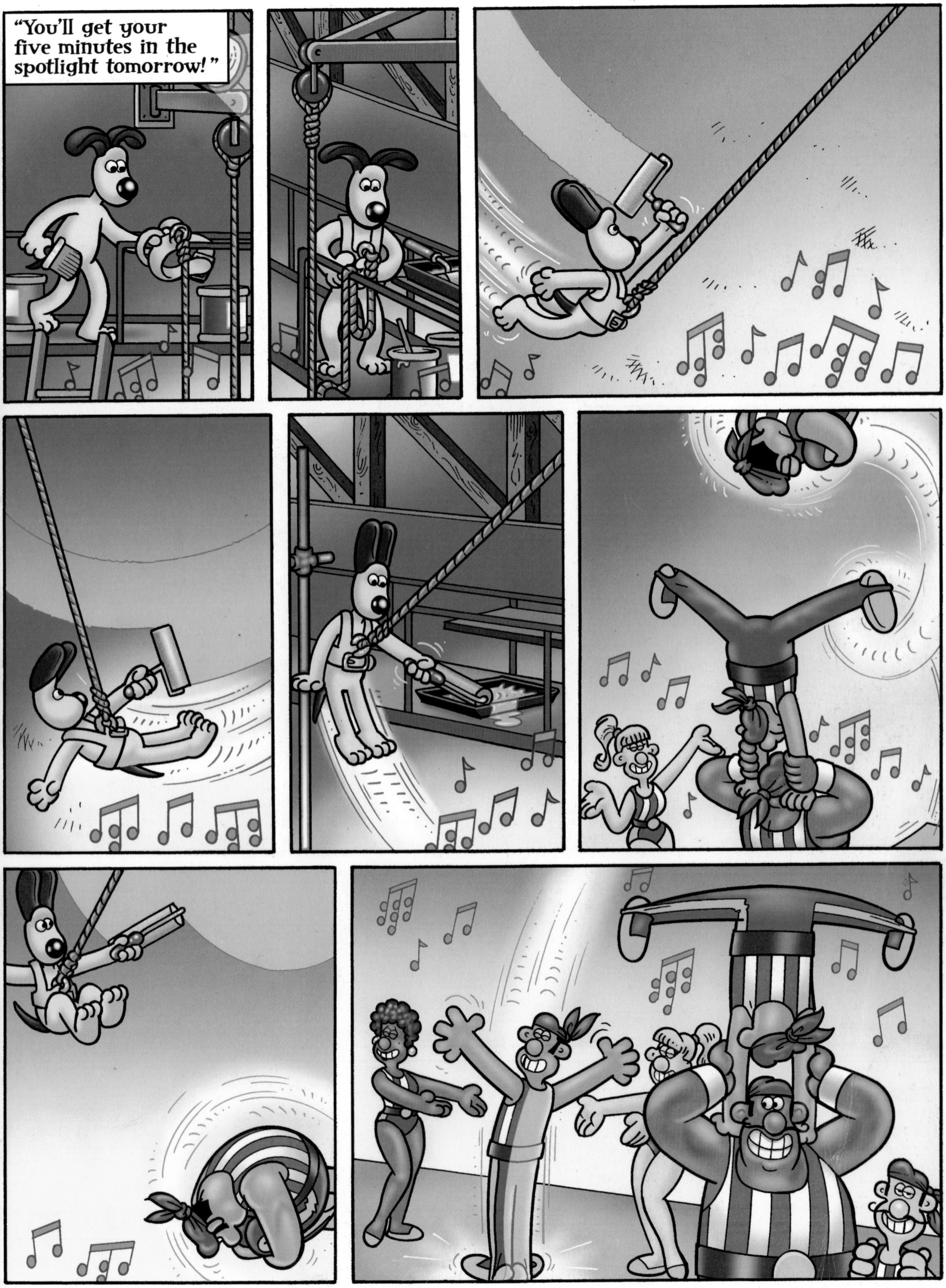
"You'll get your five minutes in the spotlight tomorrow!"

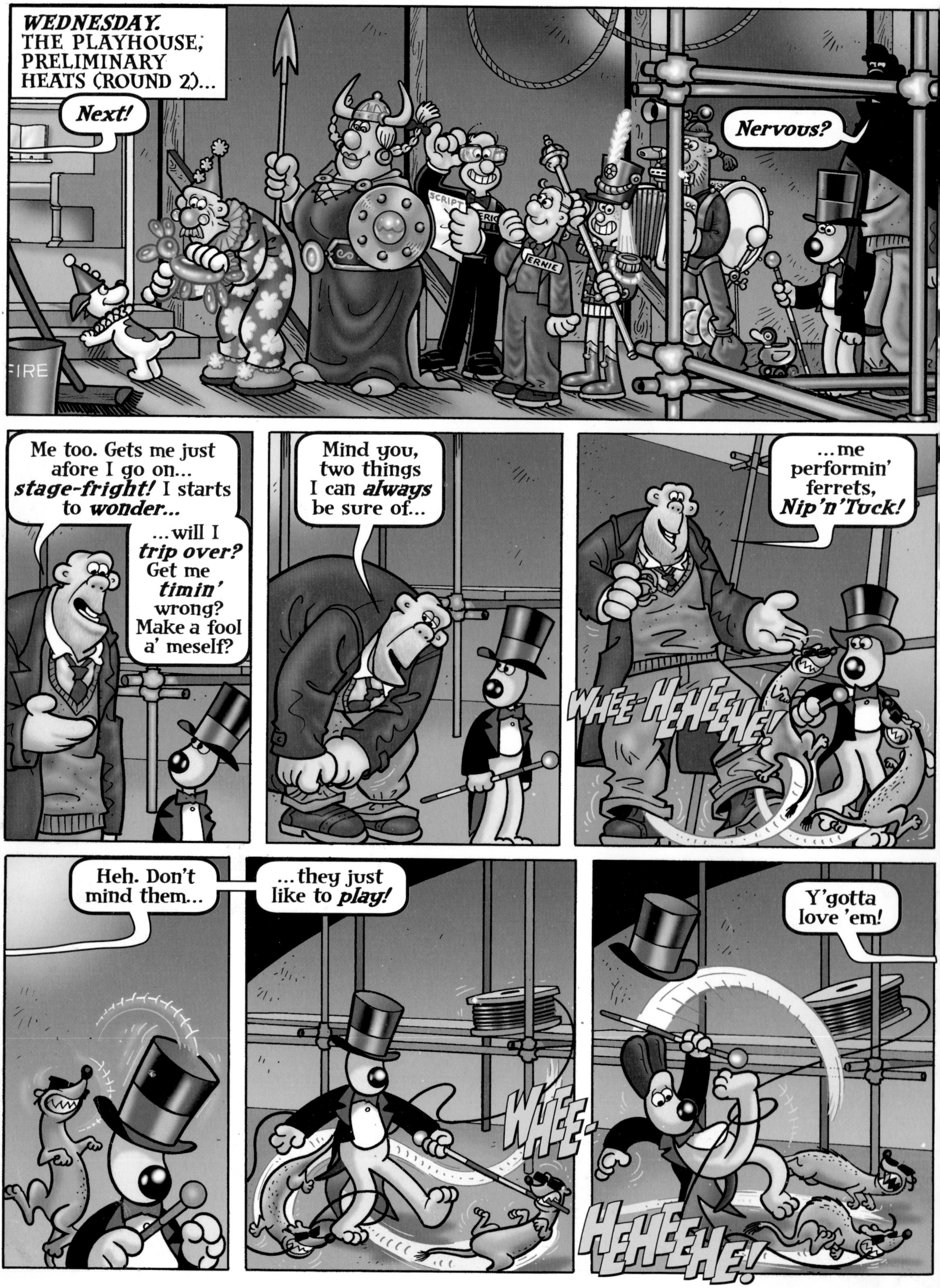

WEDNESDAY. THE PLAYHOUSE, PRELIMINARY HEATS (ROUND 2)...
Next!
FIRE
SCRIPT
ERIC
ERNIE
Nervous?
Me too. Gets me just afore I go on... stage-fright! I starts to wonder...
...will I trip over? Get me timin' wrong? Make a fool a' meself?
Mind you, two things I can always be sure of...
...me performin' ferrets, Nip'n'Tuck!
WHEE-HEHEEHE!
Heh. Don't mind them...
...they just like to play!
WHEE-
Y'gotta love 'em!
HEHEEHE!

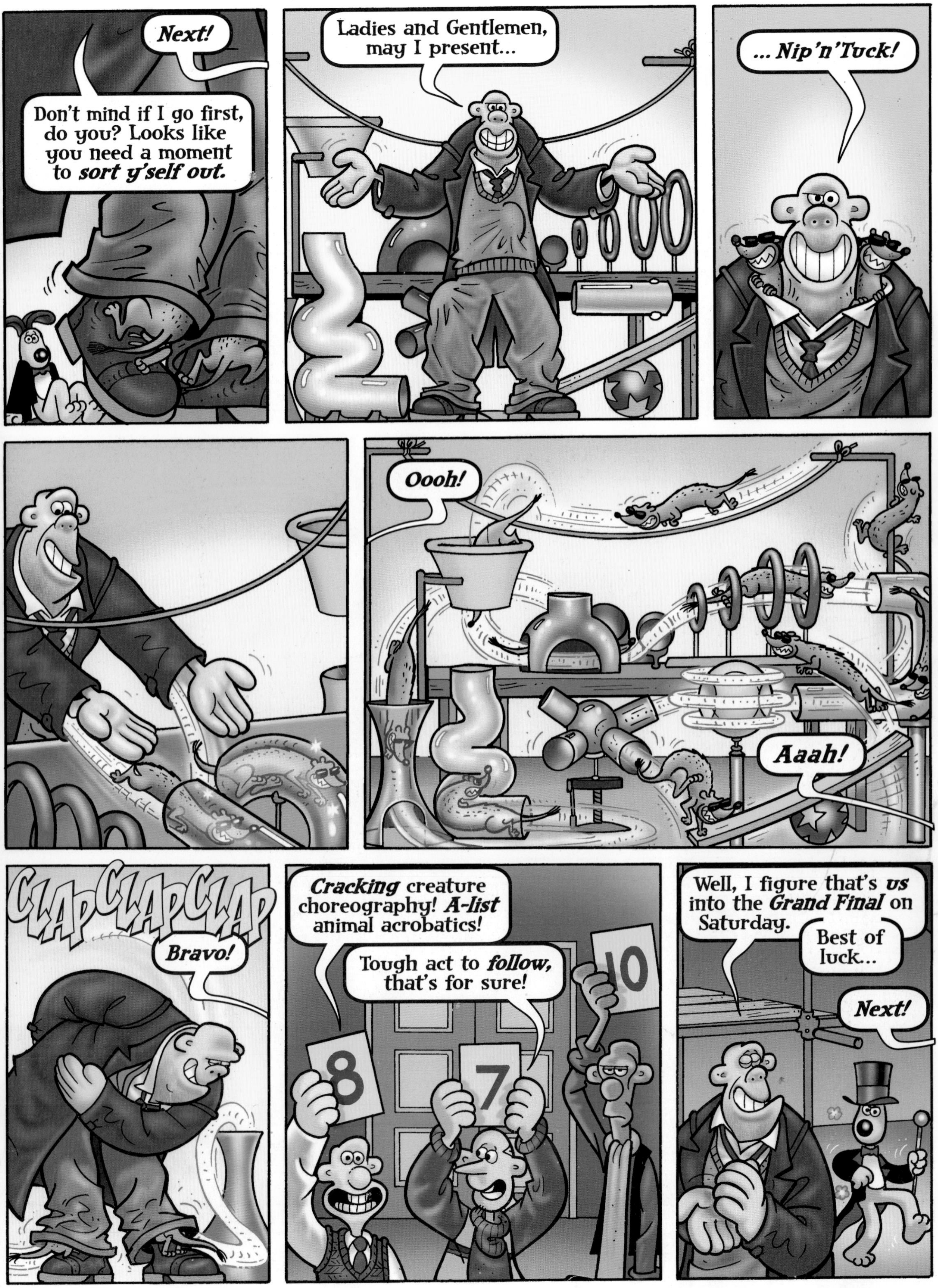
Next!
Don't mind if I go first, do you? Looks like you need a moment to *sort y'self out.*
Ladies and Gentlemen, may I present...
... Nip'n'Tuck!
Oooh!
Aaah!
CLAP CLAP CLAP
Bravo!
Cracking creature choreography! *A-list* animal acrobatics!
Tough act to *follow,* that's for sure!
8
7
10
Well, I figure that's *us* into the *Grand Final* on Saturday.
Best of luck...
Next!

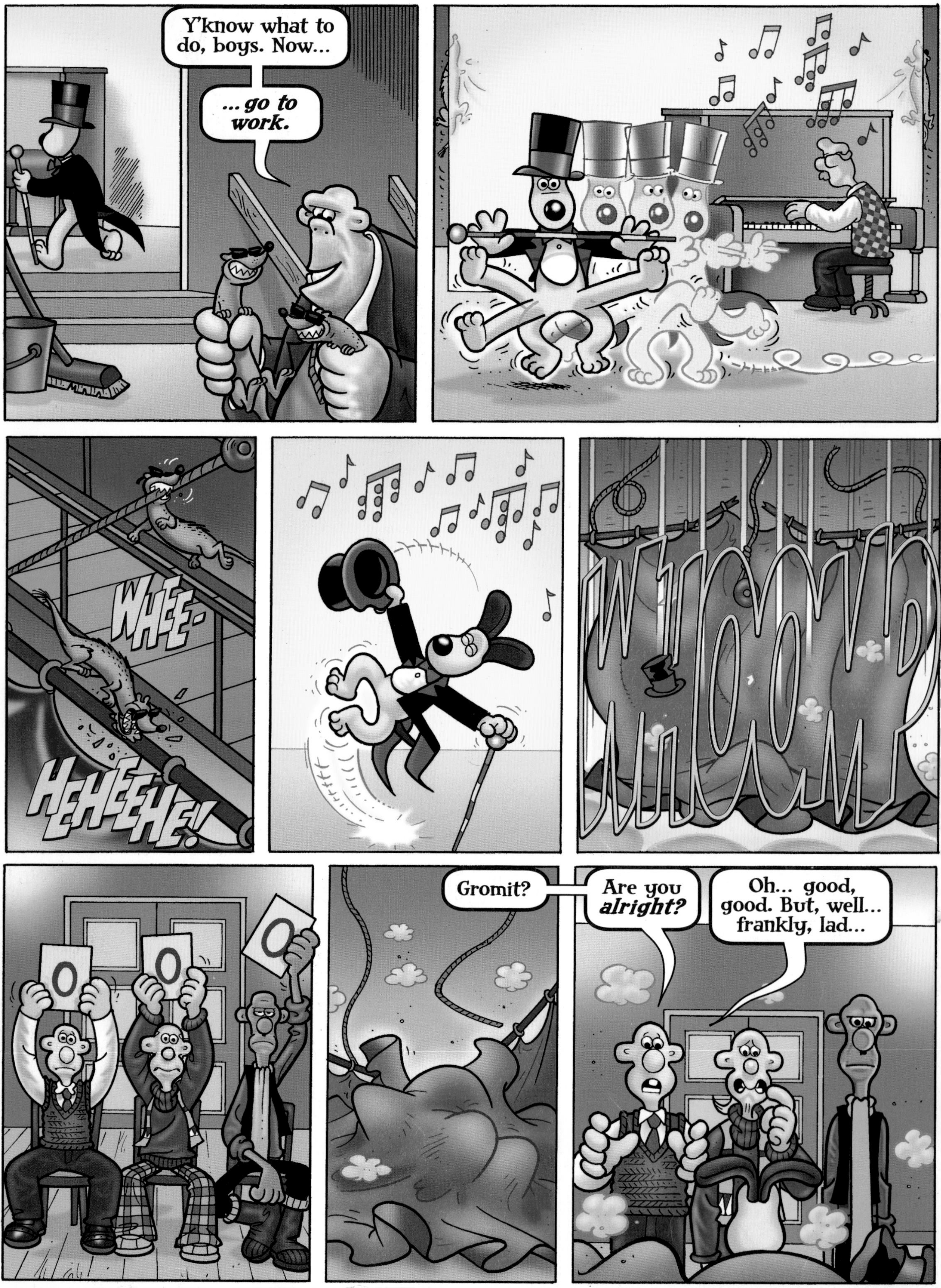
Y'know what to do, boys. Now...
...go to work.
WHEE-
HEHEEHE!
WHOOMP
0
0
0
Gromit?
Are you alright?
Oh... good, good. But, well... frankly, lad...

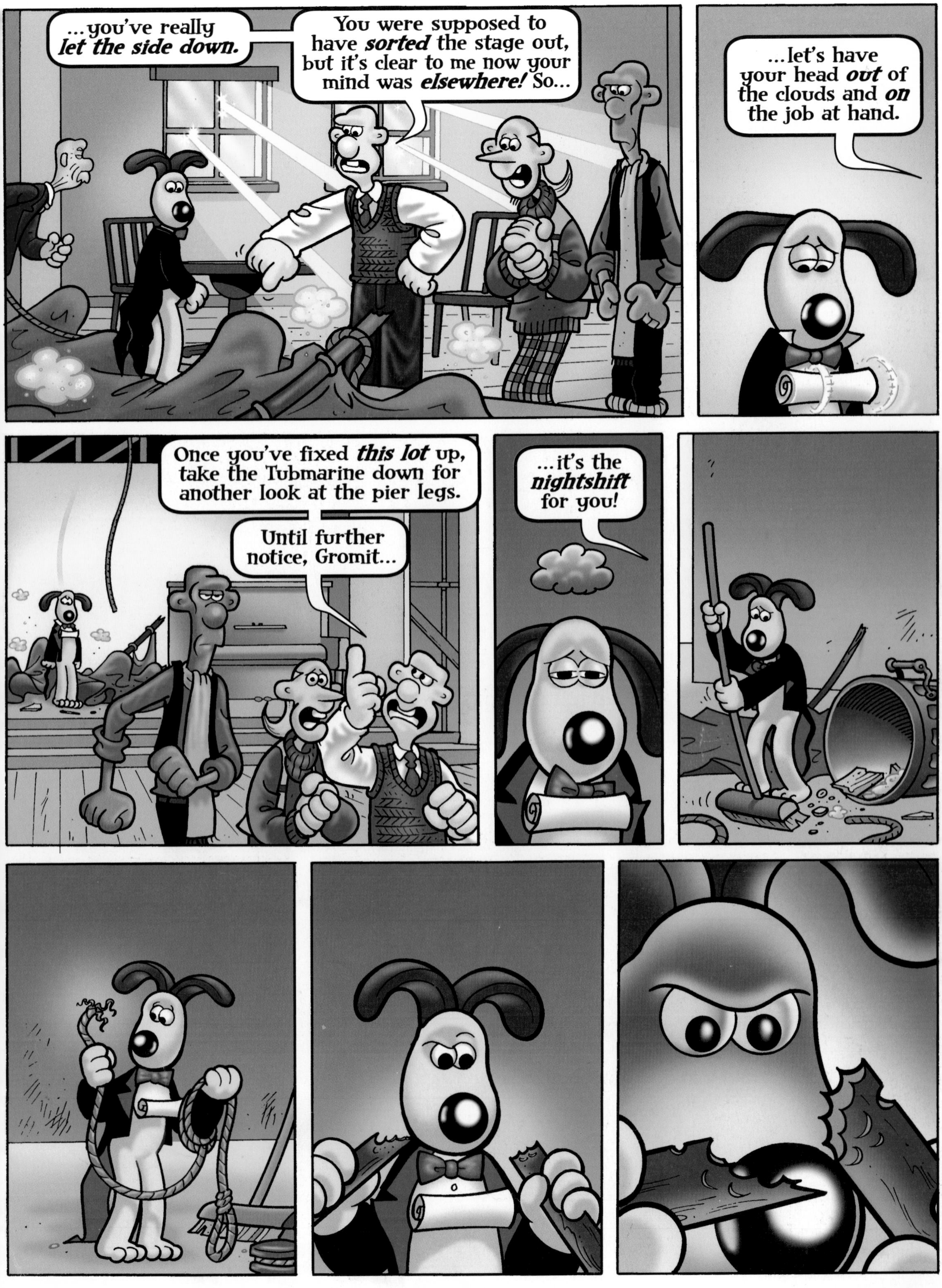

...you've really *let the side down.*
You were supposed to have *sorted* the stage out, but it's clear to me now your mind was *elsewhere!* So...
...let's have your head *out* of the clouds and *on* the job at hand.
Once you've fixed *this lot* up, take the Tubmarine down for another look at the pier legs.
Until further notice, Gromit...
...it's the *nightshift* for you!

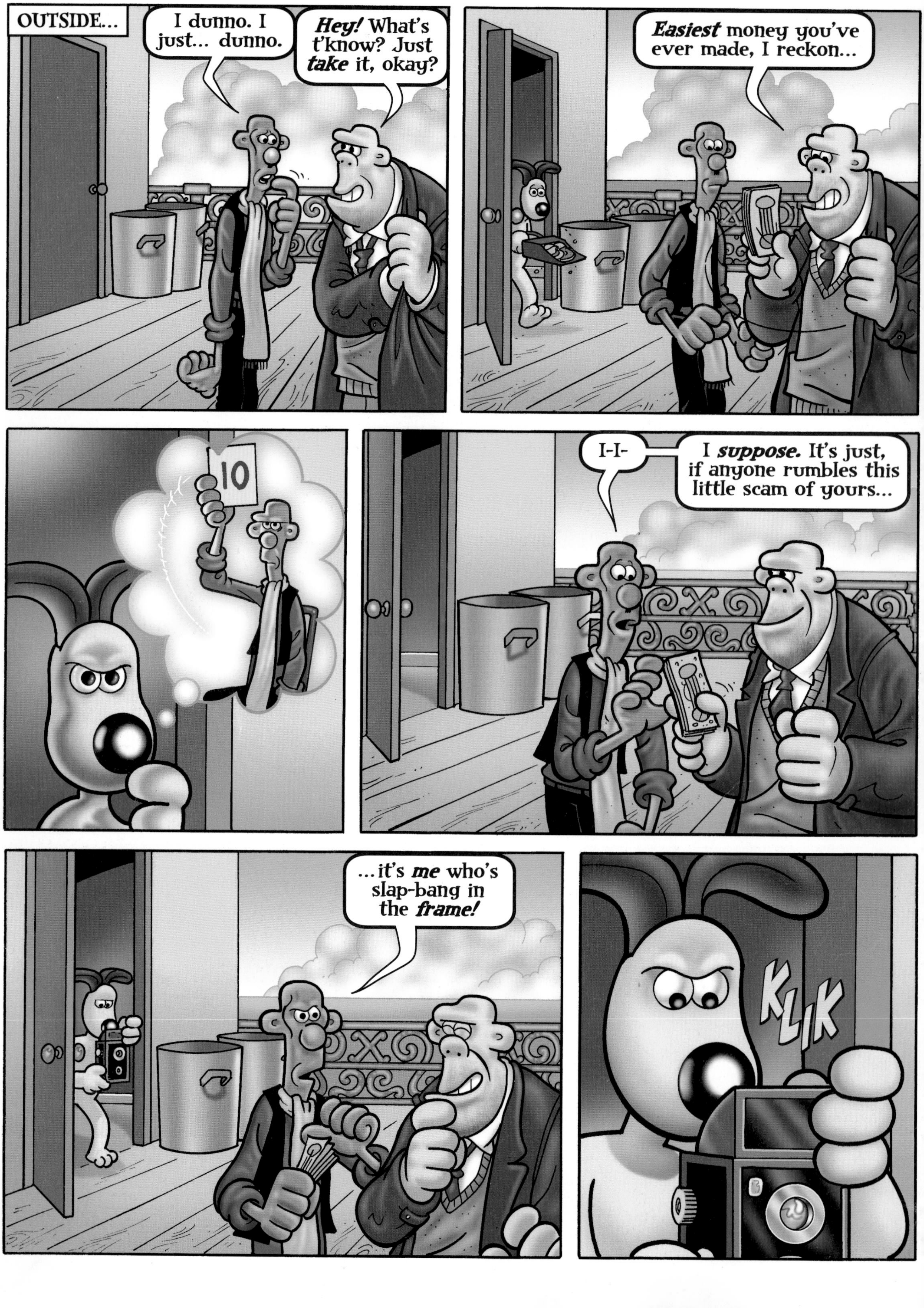

OUTSIDE...
I dunno. I just... dunno.
Hey! What's t'know? Just take it, okay?
Easiest money you've ever made, I reckon...
10
I-I-
I suppose. It's just, if anyone rumbles this little scam of yours...
...it's me who's slap-bang in the frame!
KLIK

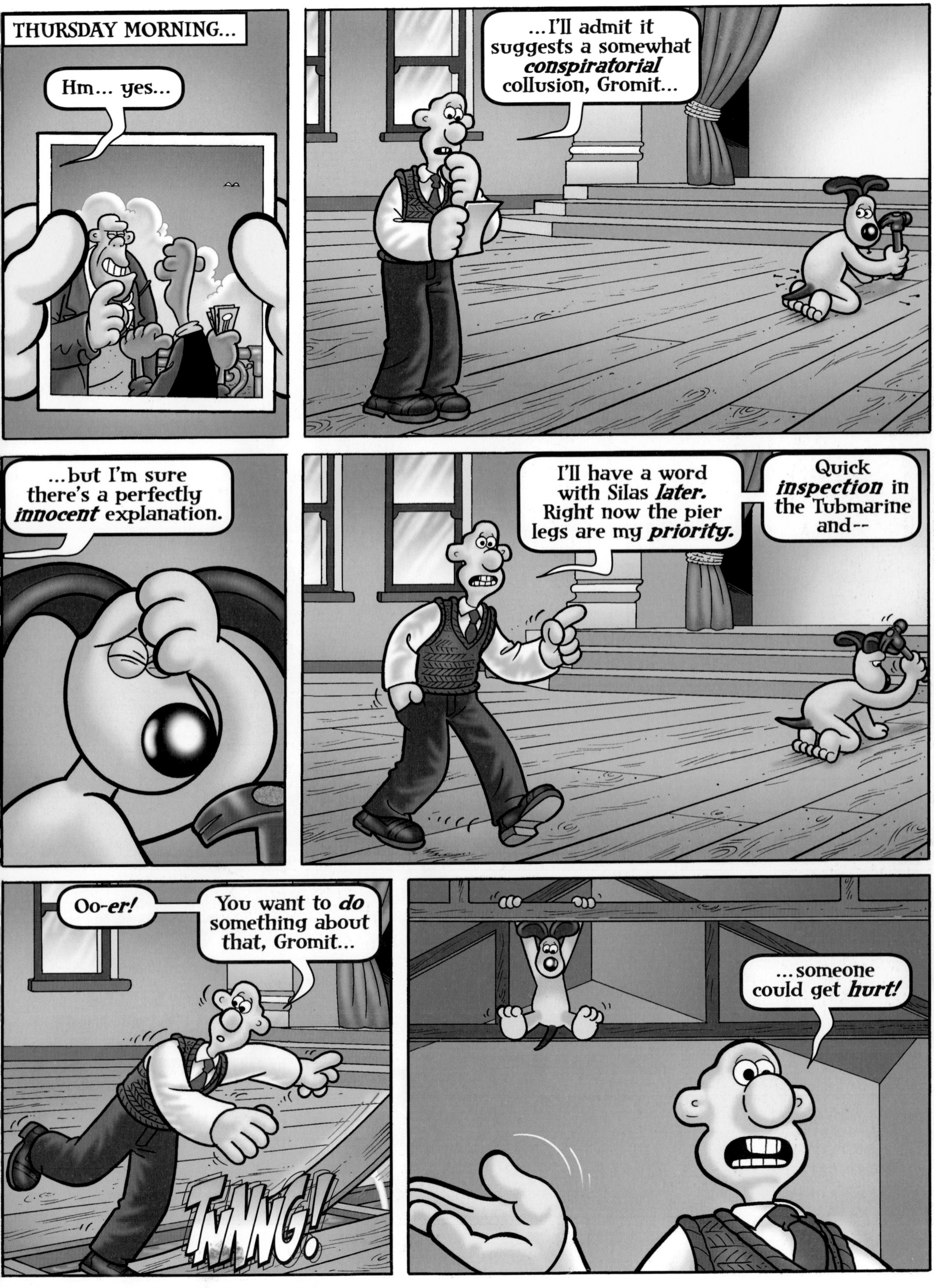
THURSDAY MORNING...
Hm... yes...
...I'll admit it suggests a somewhat *conspiratorial* collusion, Gromit...
...but I'm sure there's a perfectly *innocent* explanation.
I'll have a word with Silas *later.* Right now the pier legs are my *priority.*
Quick *inspection* in the Tubmarine and--
Oo-*er!*
You want to *do* something about that, Gromit...
TWANG!
...someone could get *hurt!*

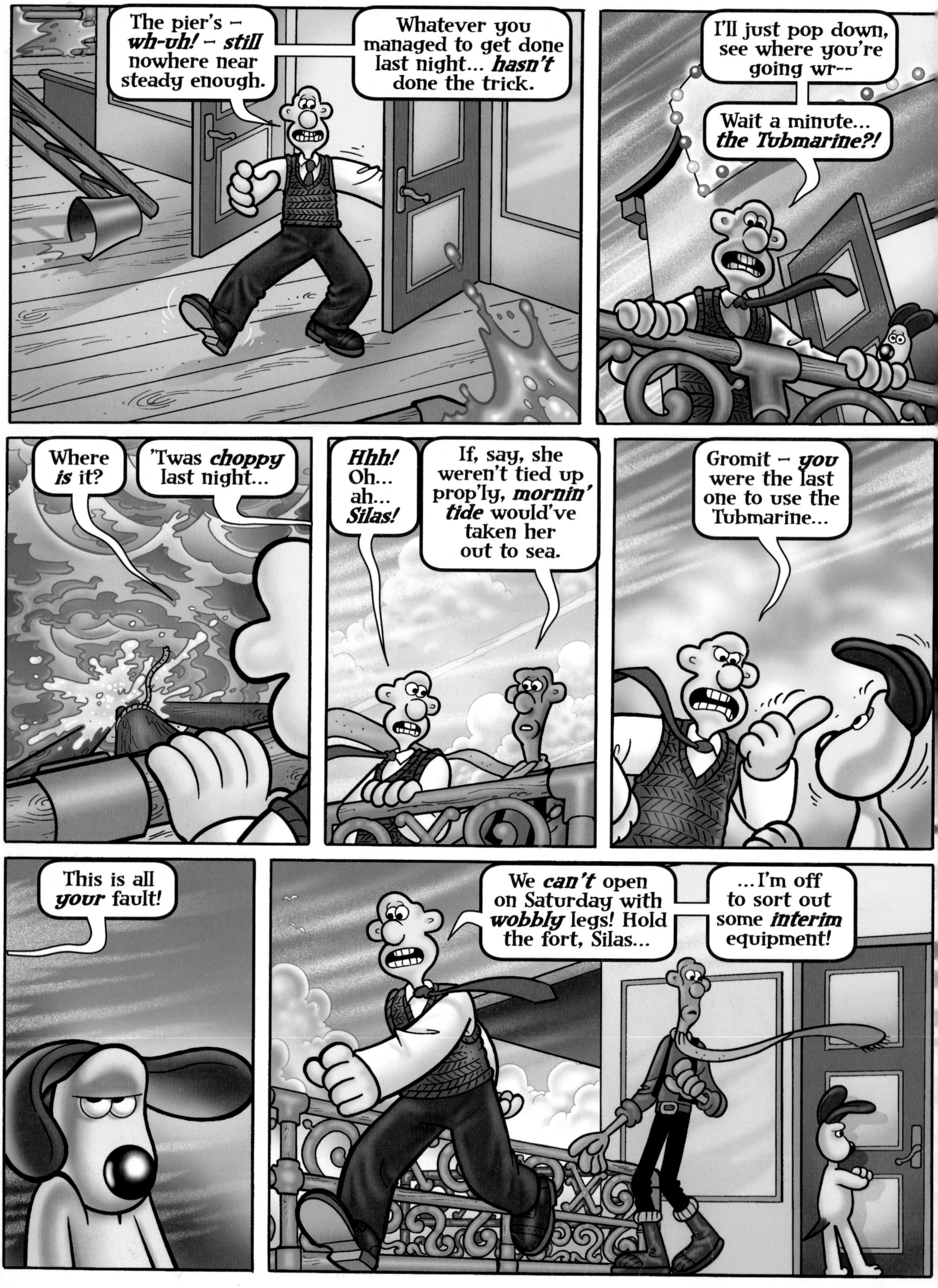
The pier's – *wh-uh!* – *still* nowhere near steady enough.
Whatever you managed to get done last night... *hasn't* done the trick.
I'll just pop down, see where you're going wr--
Wait a minute... *the Tubmarine?!*
Where *is* it?
'Twas *choppy* last night...
Hhh! Oh... ah... *Silas!*
If, say, she weren't tied up prop'ly, *mornin' tide* would've taken her out to sea.
Gromit – *you* were the last one to use the Tubmarine...
This is all *your* fault!
We *can't* open on Saturday with *wobbly* legs! Hold the fort, Silas...
...I'm off to sort out some *interim* equipment!

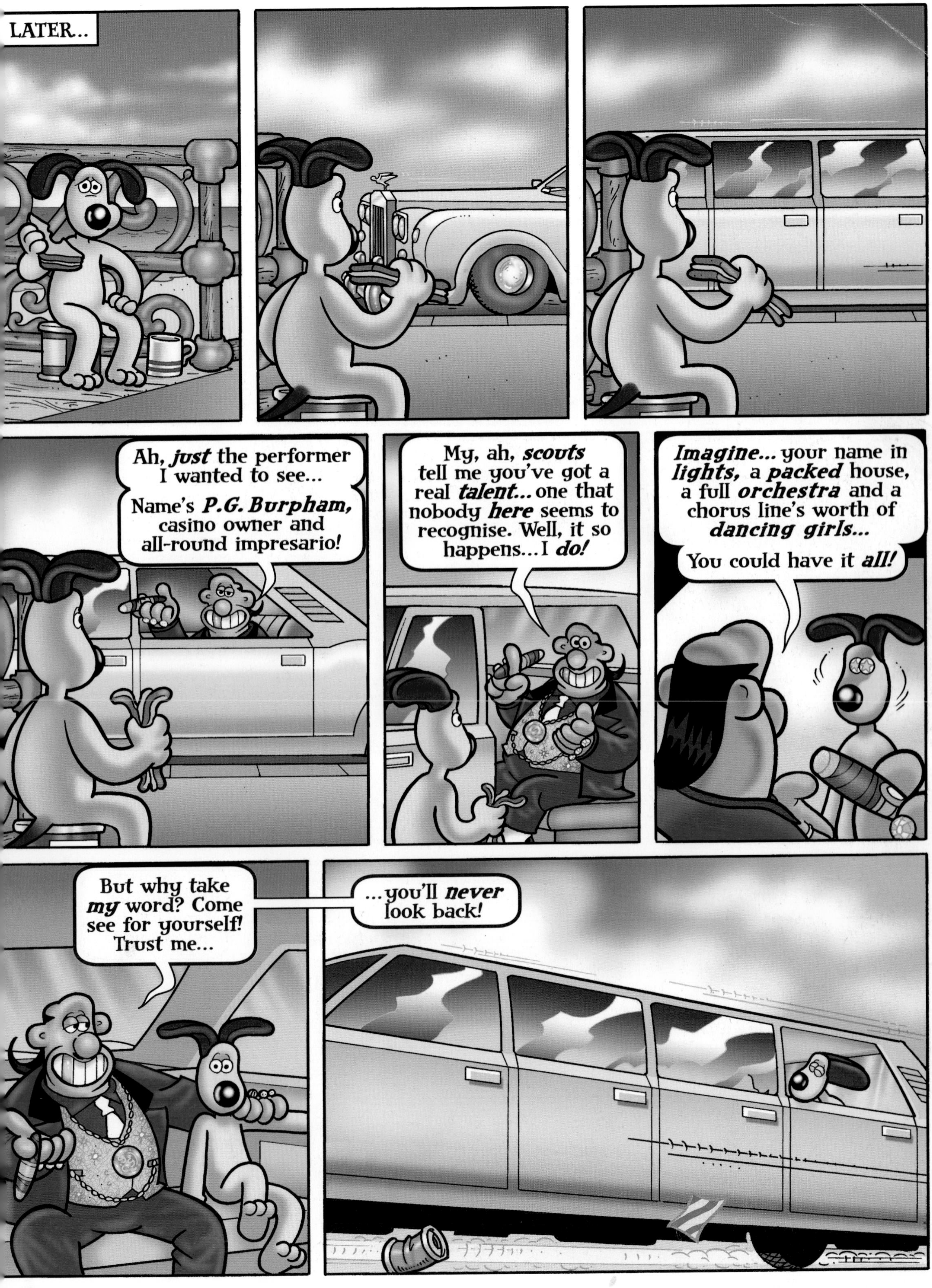
LATER...
Ah, *just* the performer I wanted to see...
Name's ***P.G. Burpham,*** casino owner and all-round impresario!
My, ah, ***scouts*** tell me you've got a real ***talent...*** one that nobody ***here*** seems to recognise. Well, it so happens... I ***do!***
Imagine... your name in ***lights,*** a ***packed*** house, a full ***orchestra*** and a chorus line's worth of ***dancing girls...***
You could have it ***all!***
But why take ***my*** word? Come see for yourself! Trust me...
...you'll ***never*** look back!

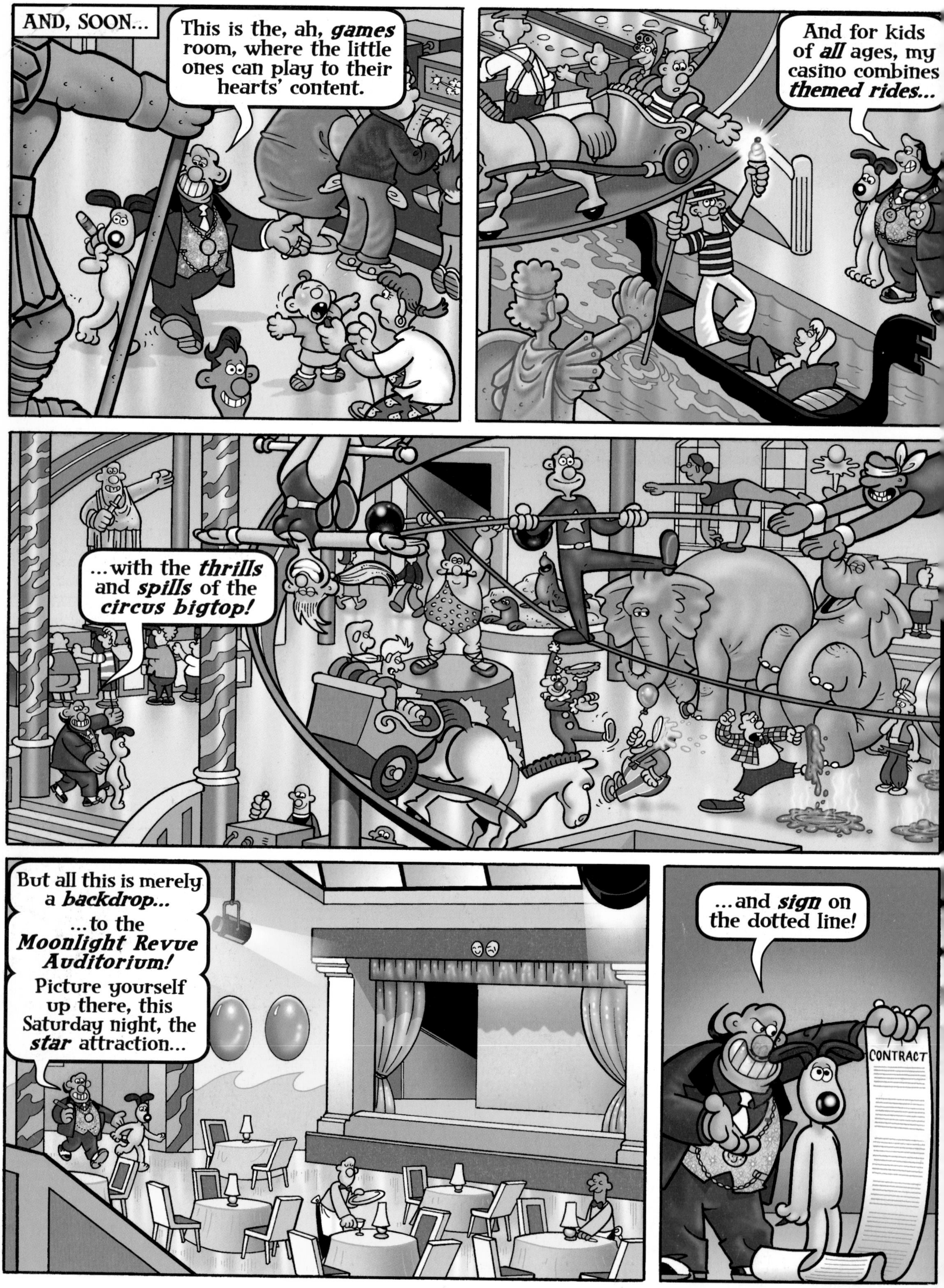
AND, SOON...
This is the, ah, *games* room, where the little ones can play to their hearts' content.
And for kids of *all* ages, my casino combines *themed rides...*
...with the *thrills* and *spills* of the *circus bigtop!*
But all this is merely a *backdrop...*
...to the *Moonlight Revue Auditorium!*
Picture yourself up there, this Saturday night, the *star* attraction...
...and *sign* on the dotted line!
CONTRACT

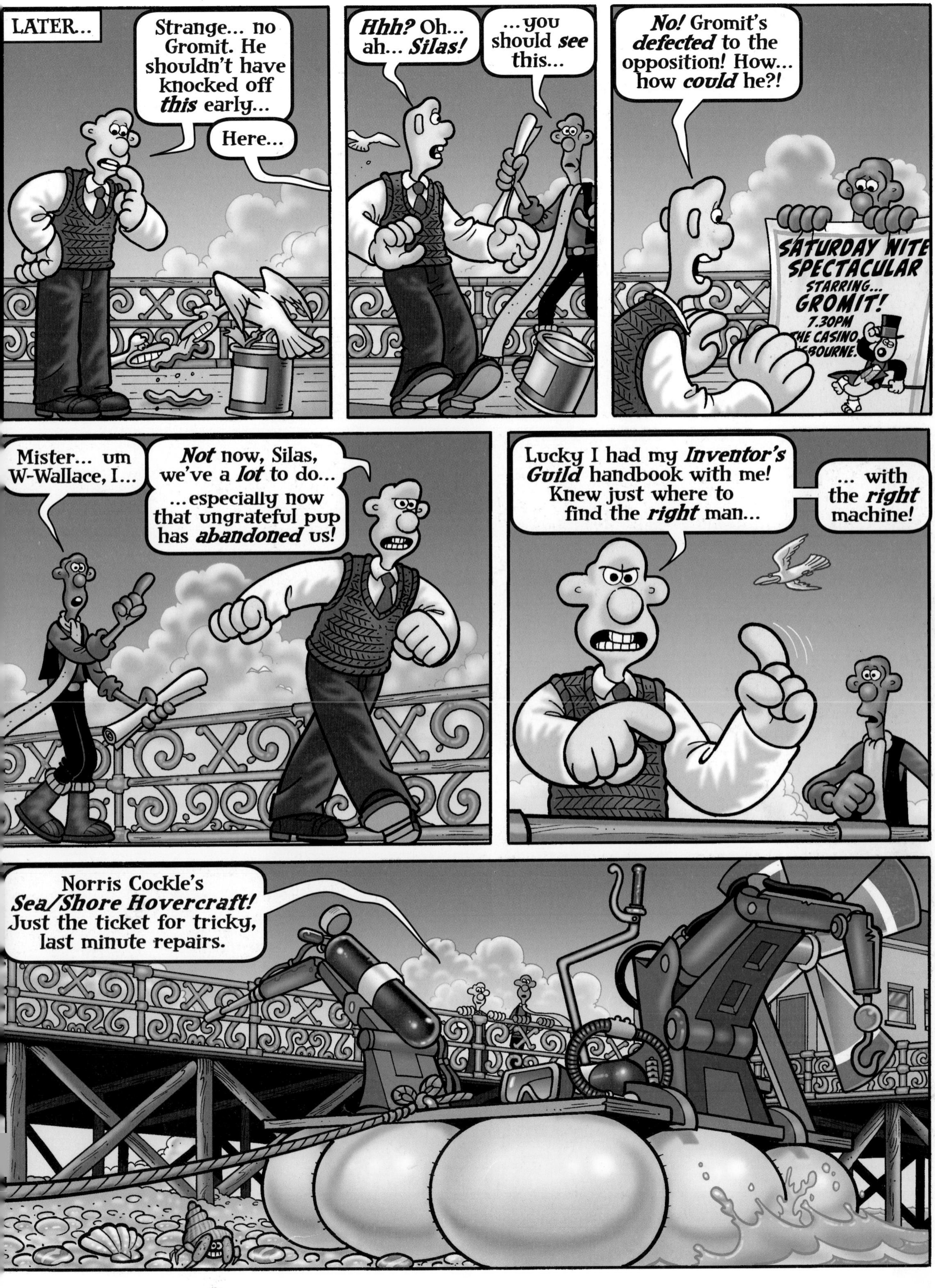

LATER...
Strange... no Gromit. He shouldn't have knocked off *this* early...
Here...
Hhh? Oh... ah... *Silas!*
...you should *see* this...
No! Gromit's *defected* to the opposition! How... how *could* he?!
SATURDAY NITE SPECTACULAR STARRING... GROMIT! 7.30PM THE CASINO
Mister... um W-Wallace, I...
Not now, Silas, we've a *lot* to do...
...especially now that ungrateful pup has *abandoned* us!
Lucky I had my *Inventor's Guild* handbook with me! Knew just where to find the *right* man...
... with the *right* machine!
Norris Cockle's *Sea/Shore Hovercraft!* Just the ticket for tricky, last minute repairs.

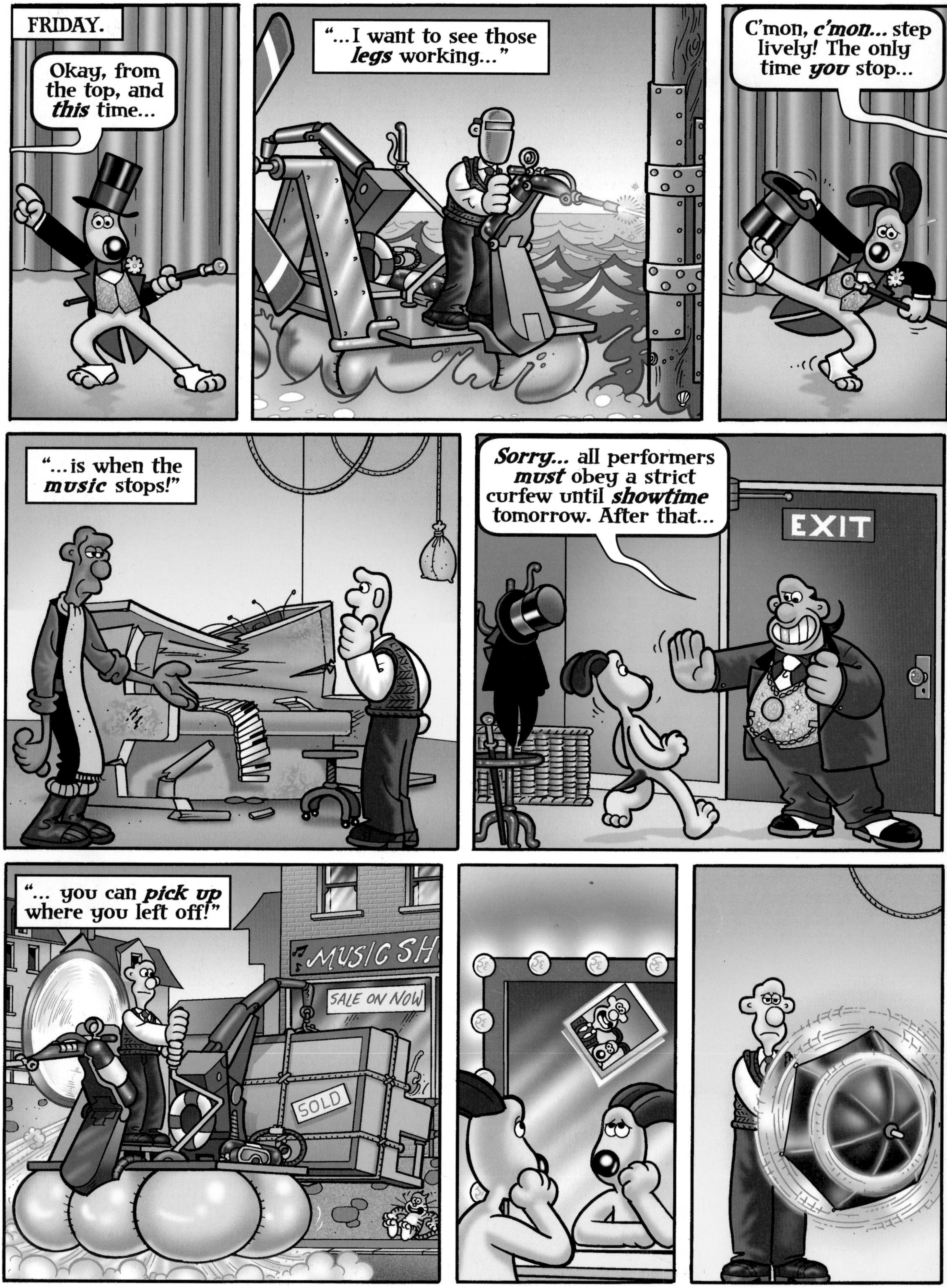
FRIDAY.
Okay, from the top, and *this* time...
"...I want to see those *legs* working..."
C'mon, *c'mon...* step lively! The only time *you* stop...
"...is when the *music* stops!"
Sorry... all performers *must* obey a strict curfew until *showtime* tomorrow. After that...
EXIT
"... you can *pick up* where you left off!"
MUSIC SH
SALE ON NOW
SOLD

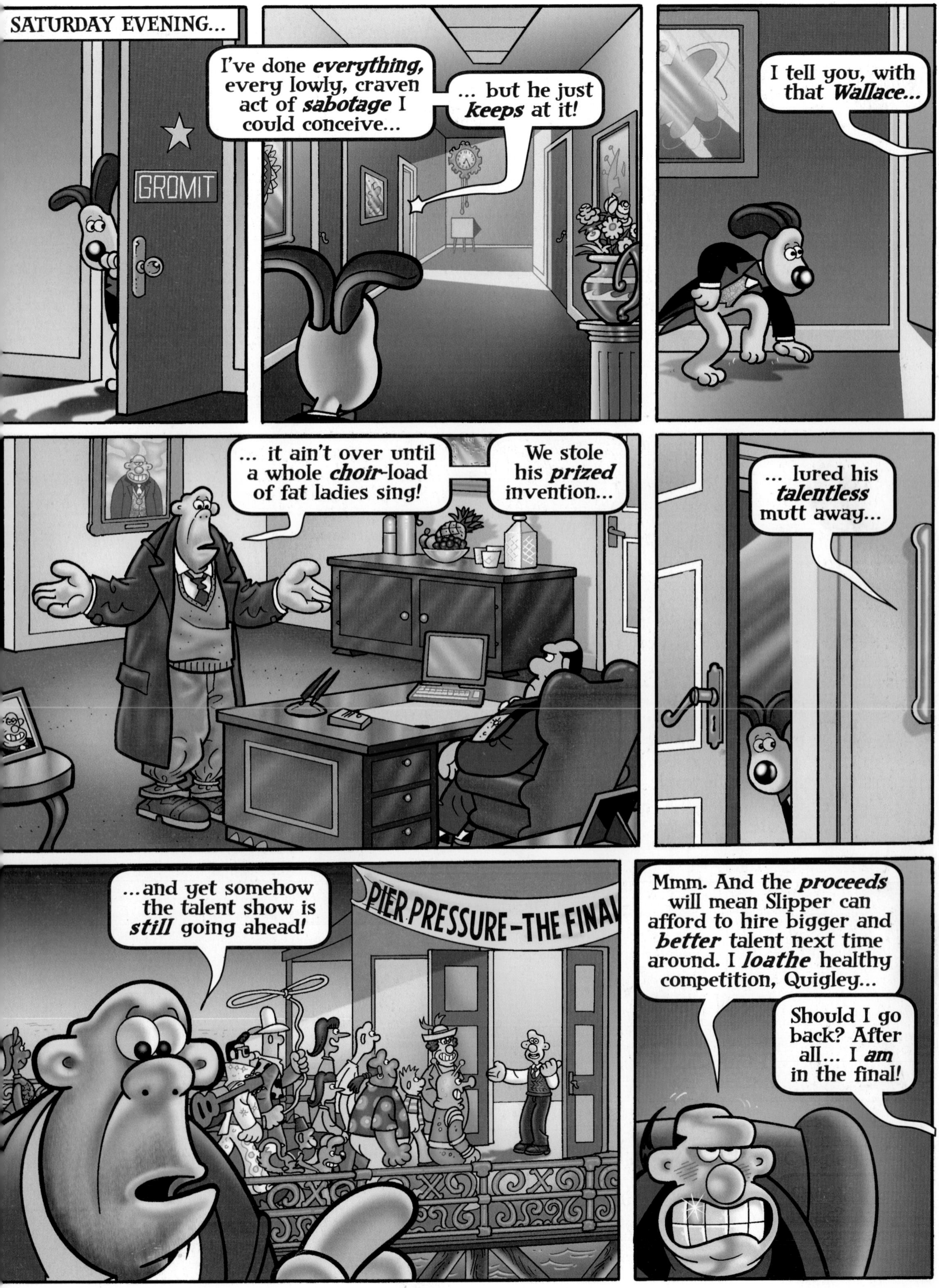
SATURDAY EVENING...
GROMIT
I've done everything, every lowly, craven act of sabotage I could conceive...
... but he just keeps at it!
I tell you, with that Wallace...
... it ain't over until a whole choir-load of fat ladies sing!
We stole his prized invention...
... lured his talentless mutt away...
...and yet somehow the talent show is still going ahead!
PIER PRESSURE–THE FINAL
Mmm. And the proceeds will mean Slipper can afford to hire bigger and better talent next time around. I loathe healthy competition, Quigley...
Should I go back? After all... I am in the final!

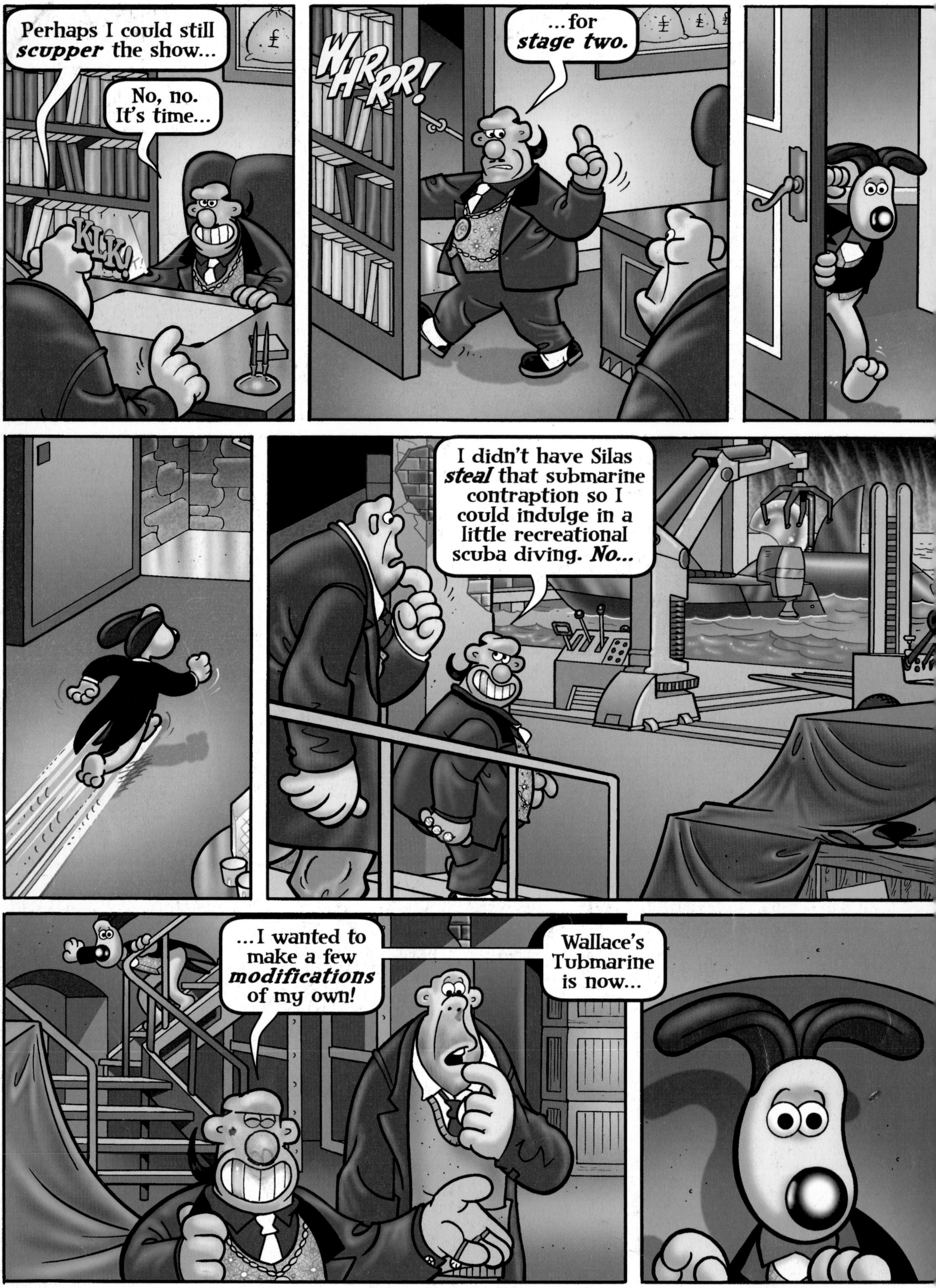

Perhaps I could still *scupper* the show...
No, no. It's time...
KLIK!
WHRRR!
...for *stage two.*
I didn't have Silas *steal* that submarine contraption so I could indulge in a little recreational scuba diving. *No...*
...I wanted to make a few *modifications* of my own!
Wallace's Tubmarine is now...

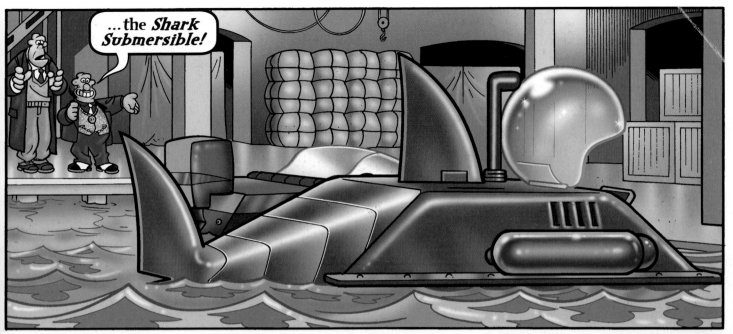

When the talent show gets underway at eight o'clock, I'll be underwater, waiting... with *torpedoes* armed and ready!

One well placed *shot*... and the pier will *literally* be on its *last legs!* They'll *have* to abandon--

TNNG!

It's that *confounded* dog! He's heard *everything!*

Get him!

Right away, Mister Burpham, sir... right away!

Boys...

...he's all *yours!*

WHEE-

HEHEEHE!

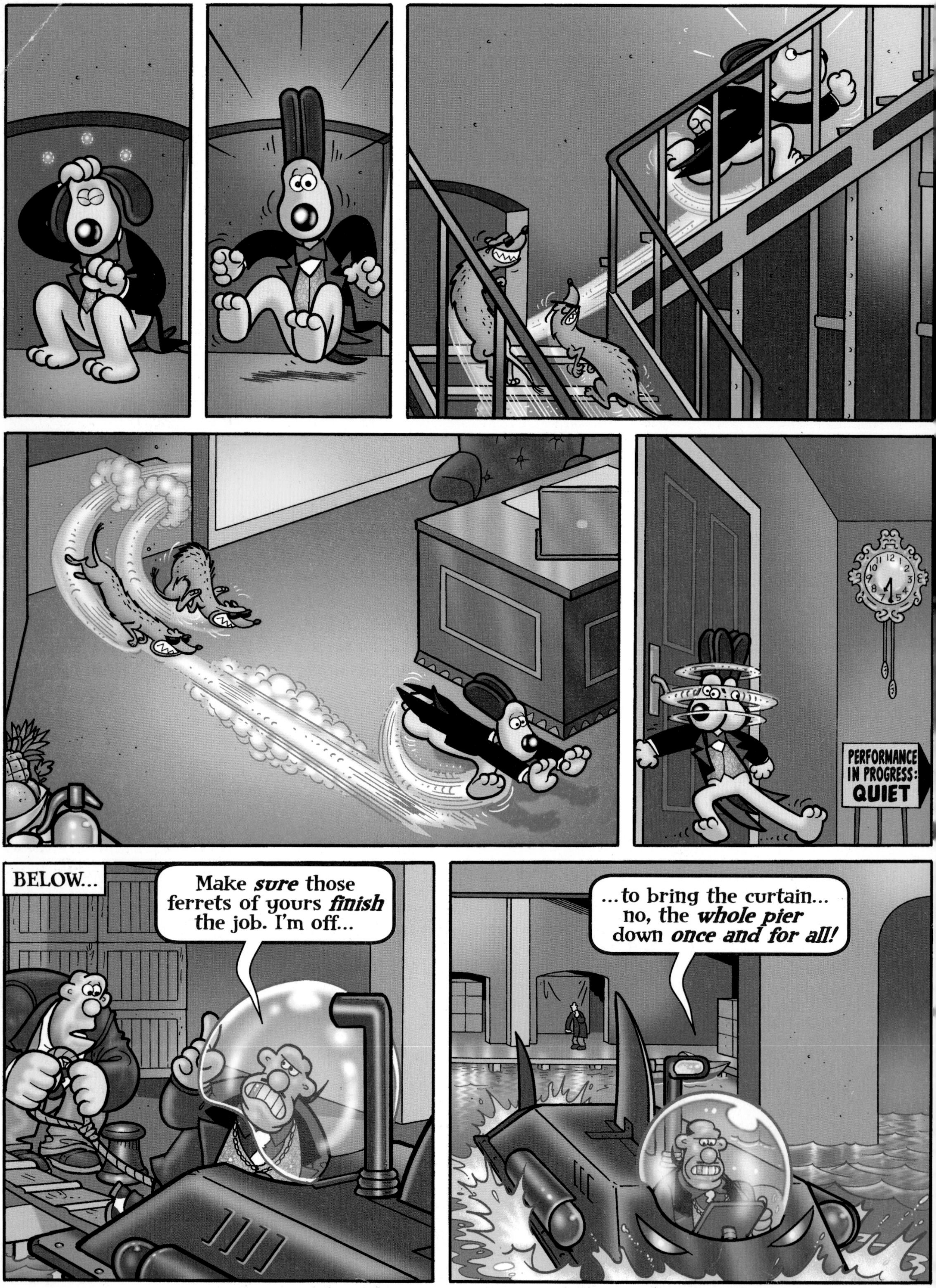

PERFORMANCE IN PROGRESS: QUIET
BELOW...
Make sure those ferrets of yours finish the job. I'm off...
...to bring the curtain... no, the whole pier down once and for all!

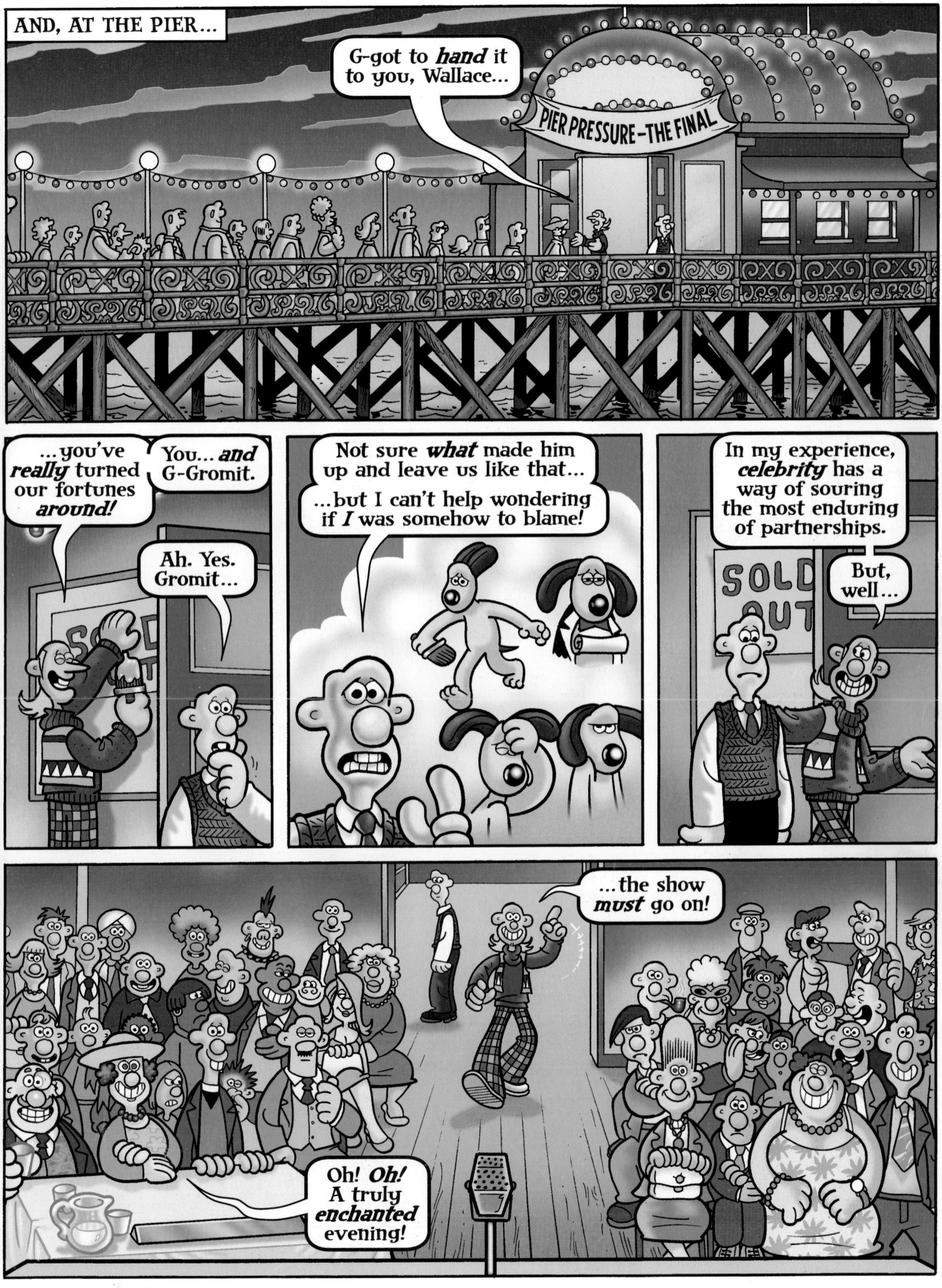
AND, AT THE PIER...
G-got to *hand* it to you, Wallace...
PIER PRESSURE – THE FINAL
...you've *really* turned our fortunes *around!*
You... *and* G-Gromit.
Ah. Yes. Gromit...
Not sure *what* made him up and leave us like that...
...but I can't help wondering if *I* was somehow to blame!
In my experience, *celebrity* has a way of souring the most enduring of partnerships.
SOLD OUT
But, well...
...the show *must* go on!
Oh! *Oh!* A truly *enchanted* evening!

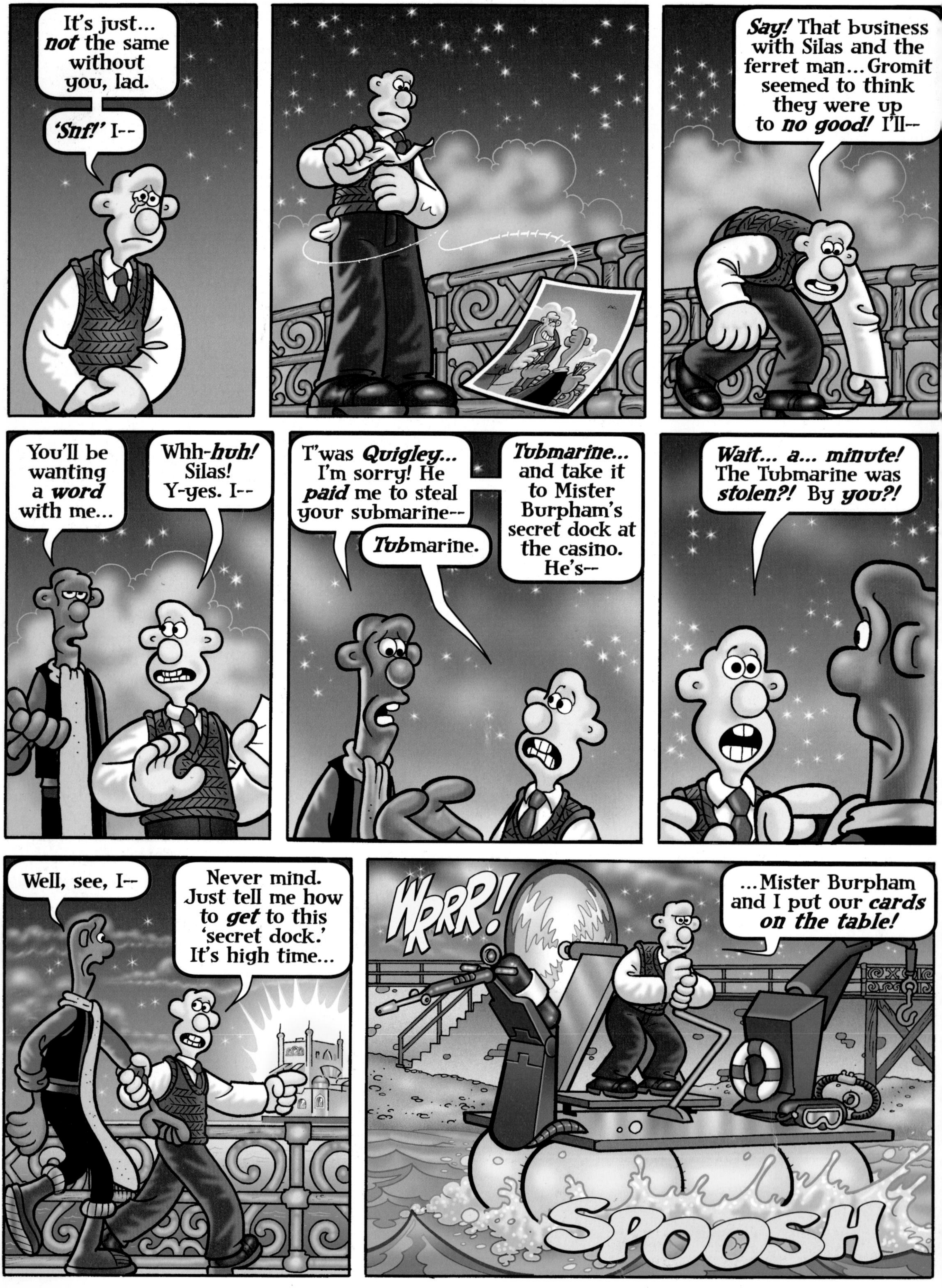
It's just... *not* the same without you, lad.
'Snf!' I--
Say! That business with Silas and the ferret man... Gromit seemed to think they were up to *no good!* I'll--
You'll be wanting a *word* with me...
Whh-*huh!* Silas! Y-yes. I--
T'was *Quigley...* I'm sorry! He *paid* me to steal your submarine--
*Tub*marine.
Tubmarine... and take it to Mister Burpham's secret dock at the casino. He's--
Wait... a... minute! The Tubmarine was *stolen?!* By *you?!*
Well, see, I--
Never mind. Just tell me how to *get* to this 'secret dock.' It's high time...
WRRR!
...Mister Burpham and I put our *cards on the table!*
SPOOSH

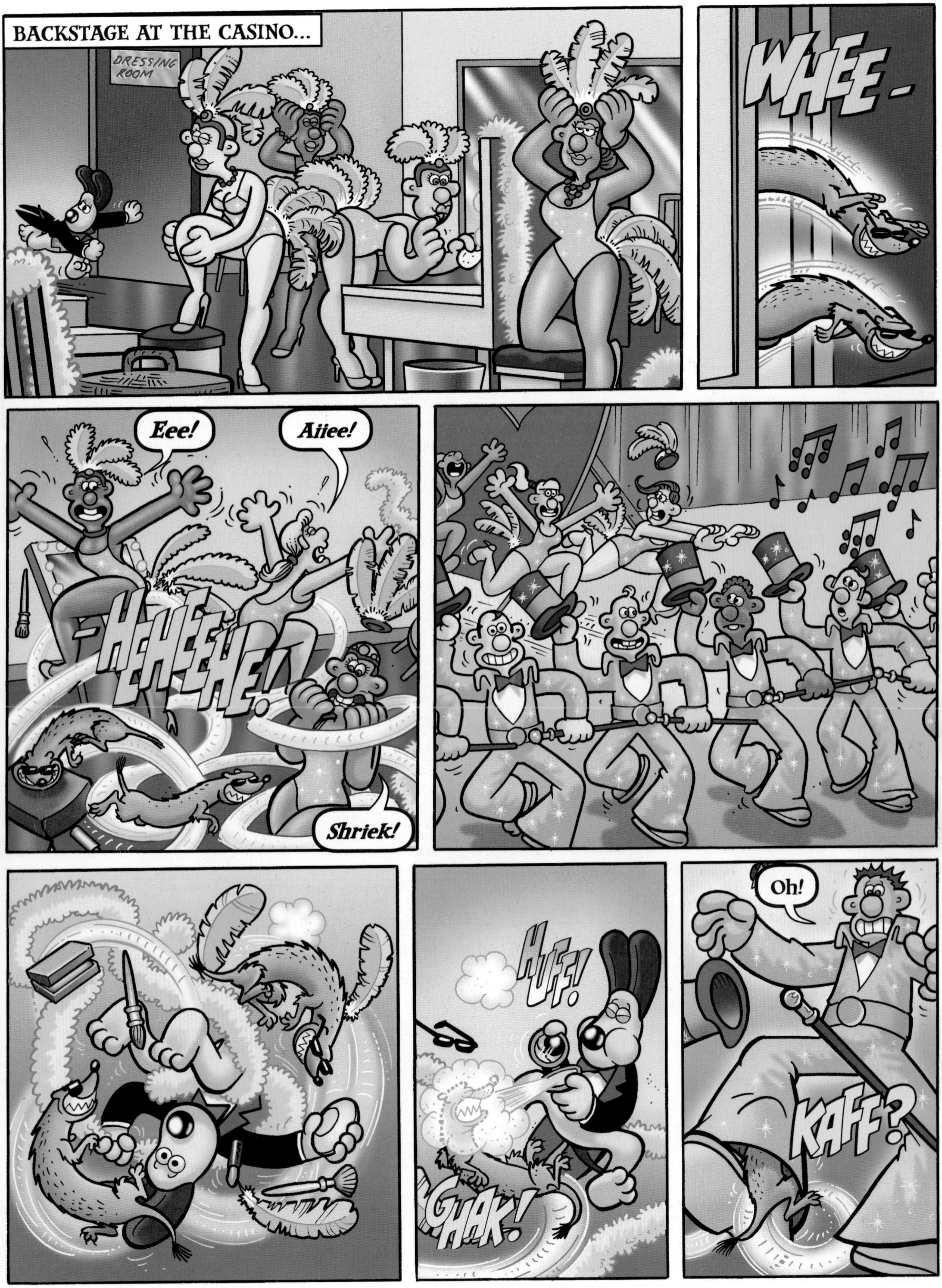

BACKSTAGE AT THE CASINO...
DRESSING ROOM
WHEE-
Eee!
Aiiee!
HEHEEHEHE!
Shriek!
HUFF!
GHAK!
Oh!
KAFF?

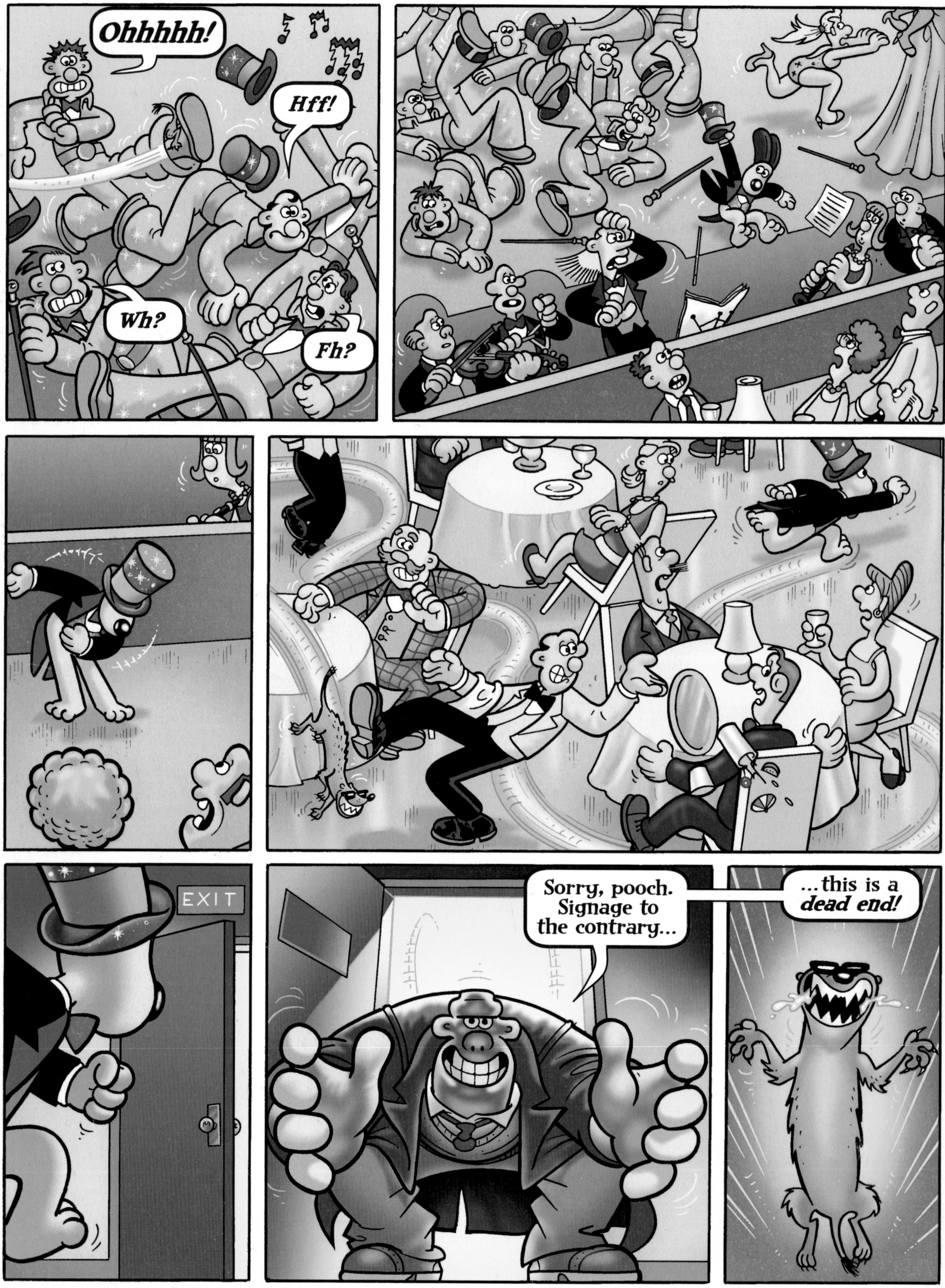
Ohhhhh!
Hff!
Wh?
Fh?
EXIT
Sorry, pooch. Signage to the contrary...
...this is a dead end!

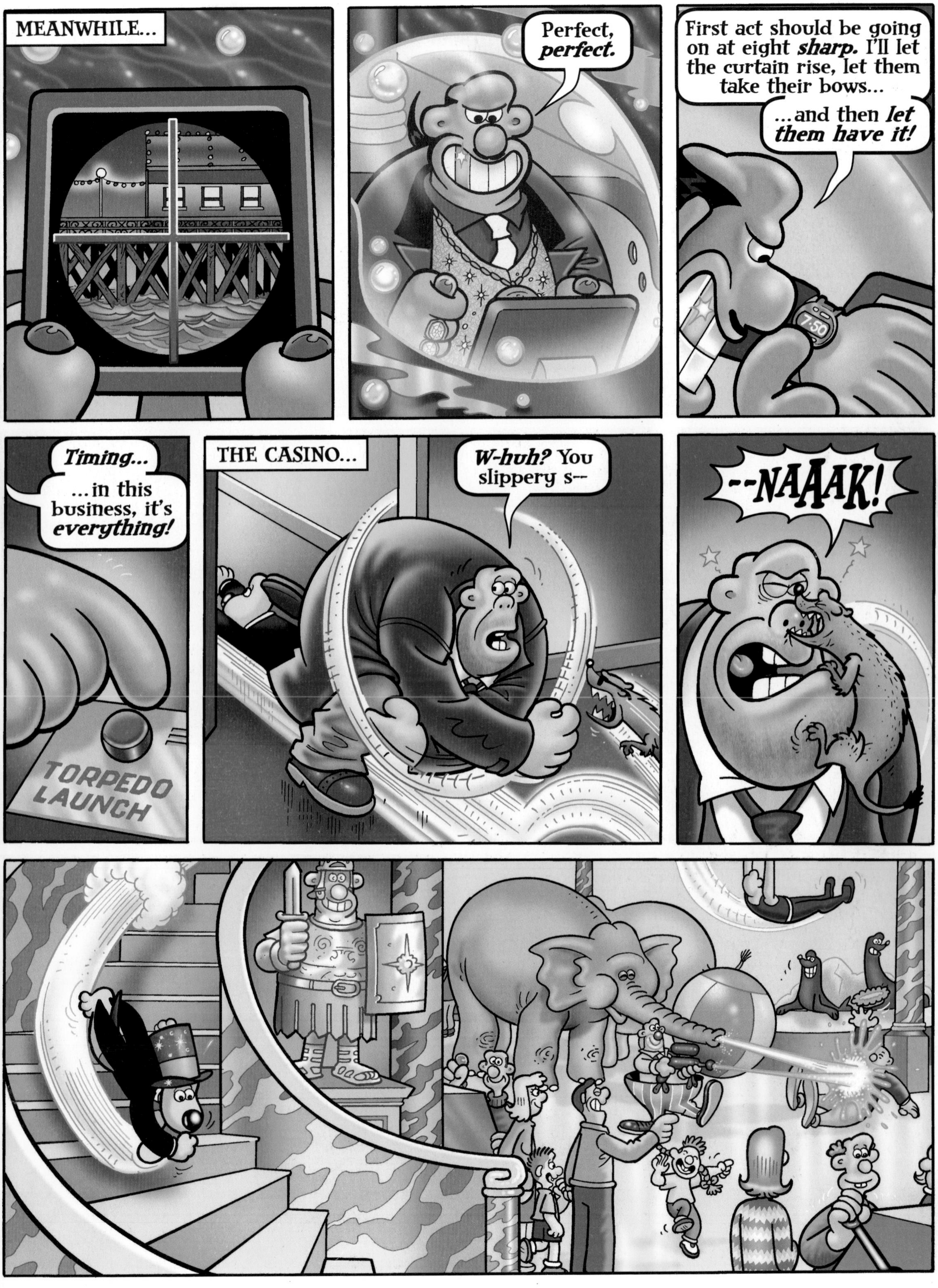
MEANWHILE...
Perfect, *perfect.*
First act should be going on at eight ***sharp.*** I'll let the curtain rise, let them take their bows...
...and then ***let them have it!***
7:50
Timing...
...in this business, it's ***everything!***
TORPEDO LAUNCH
THE CASINO...
W-huh? You slippery s--
--NAAAK!

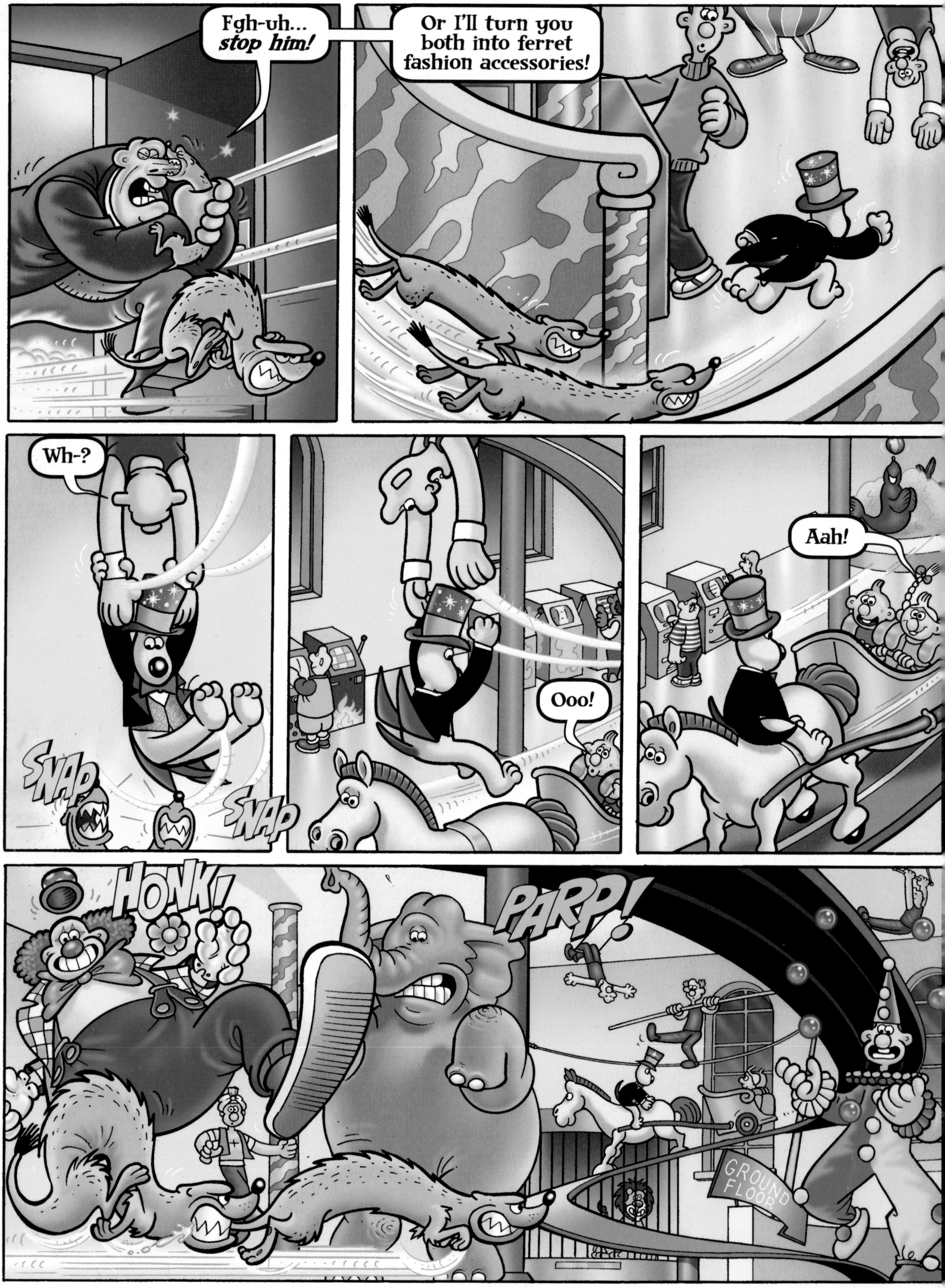
Fgh-uh... *stop him!*
Or I'll turn you both into ferret fashion accessories!
Wh-?
SNAP
SNAP
Ooo!
Aah!
HONK!
PARP!
GROUND FLOOR

OUTSIDE...

According to Silas...

...this canal system has a 'staff only' tributary, leading to--

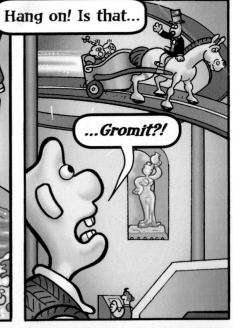

Hang on! Is that...

...Gromit?!

And Quigley! What's going--

Hh! Low bridge!

CLIK!

CLIK!

WRRR!

Phew! Almost got an early ba--

BUMP

Ooo... sorry!

SPOSSH

It-it looks like Gromit's in a *spot of bother!*

Hang on, lad...

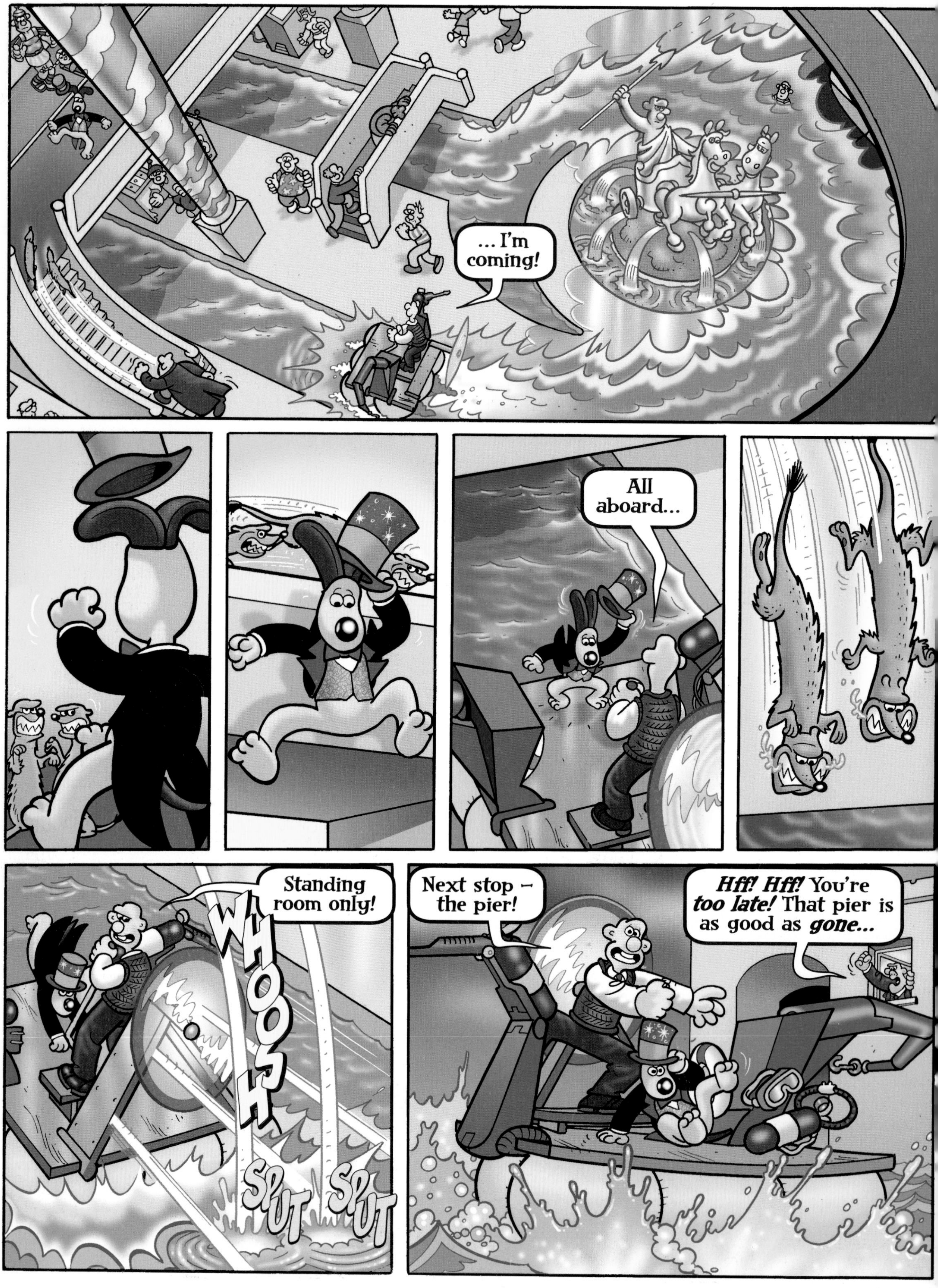

... I'm coming!
All aboard...
Standing room only!
WHOOOSH
SPUT SPUT
Next stop – the pier!
Hff! Hff! You're too late! That pier is as good as gone...

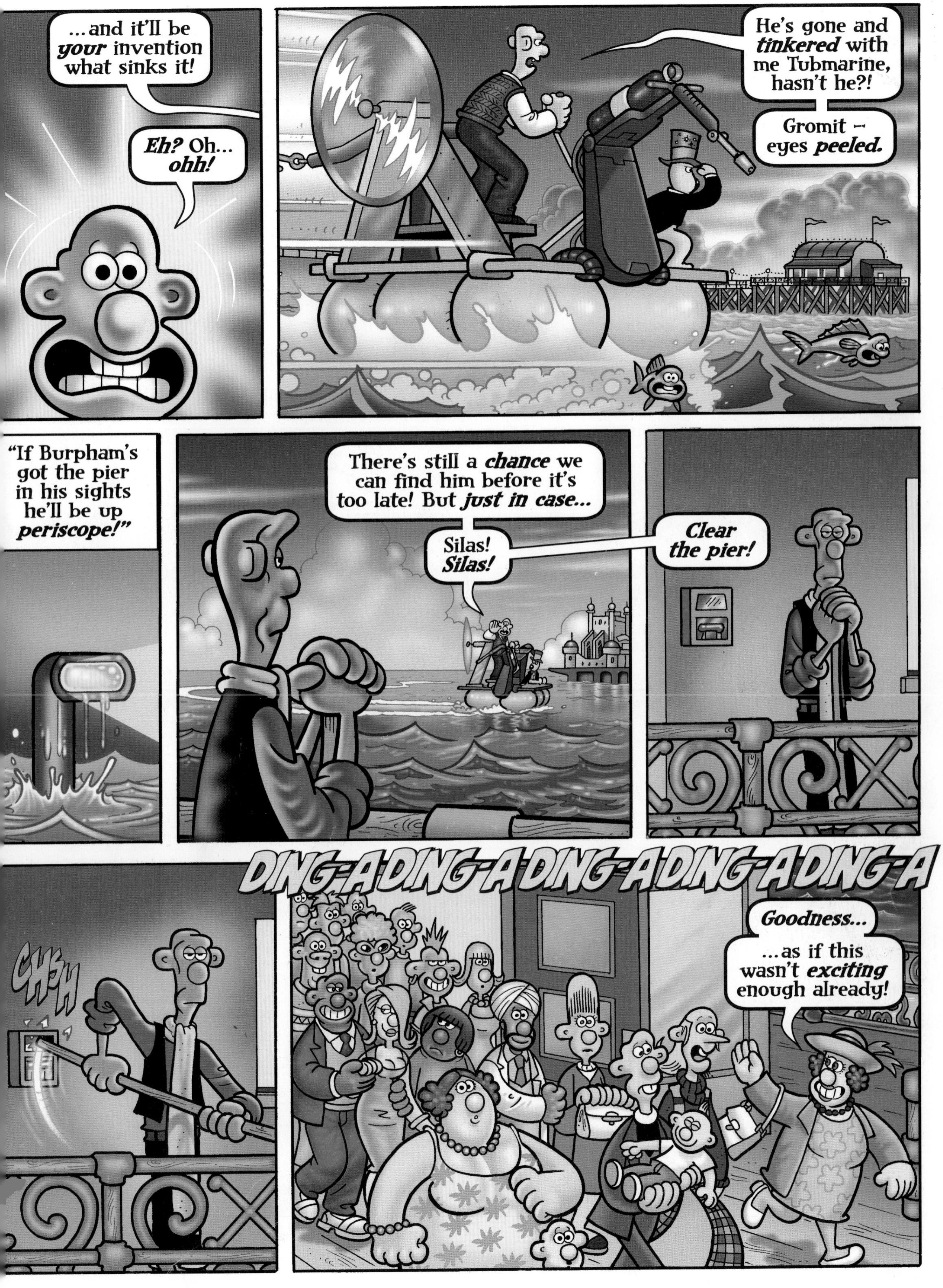

...and it'll be *your* invention what sinks it!
Eh? Oh... *ohh!*
He's gone and *tinkered* with me Tubmarine, hasn't he?!
Gromit – eyes *peeled.*
"If Burpham's got the pier in his sights he'll be up *periscope!"*
There's still a *chance* we can find him before it's too late! But *just in case...*
Silas! *Silas!*
Clear the pier!
CHSH
DING-A DING-A DING-A DING-A DING-A
Goodness...
...as if this wasn't *exciting* enough already!

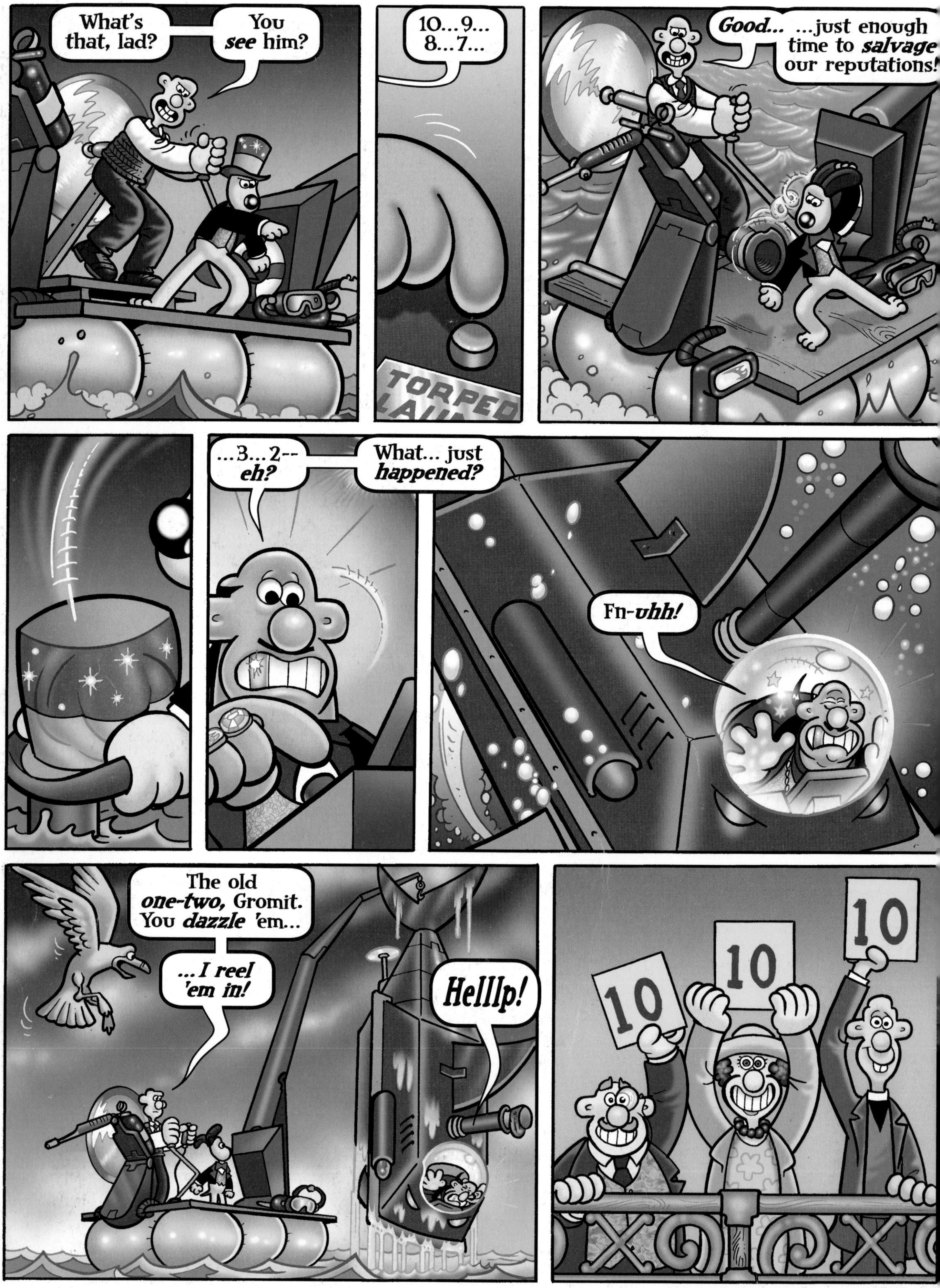
What's that, lad?
You *see* him?
10...9...
8...7...
TORPED
Good... ...just enough time to *salvage* our reputations!
...3...2--
eh?
What... just *happened?*
Fn-*uhh!*
The old *one-two,* Gromit. You *dazzle* 'em...
...I reel 'em in!
Helllp!
10
10
10

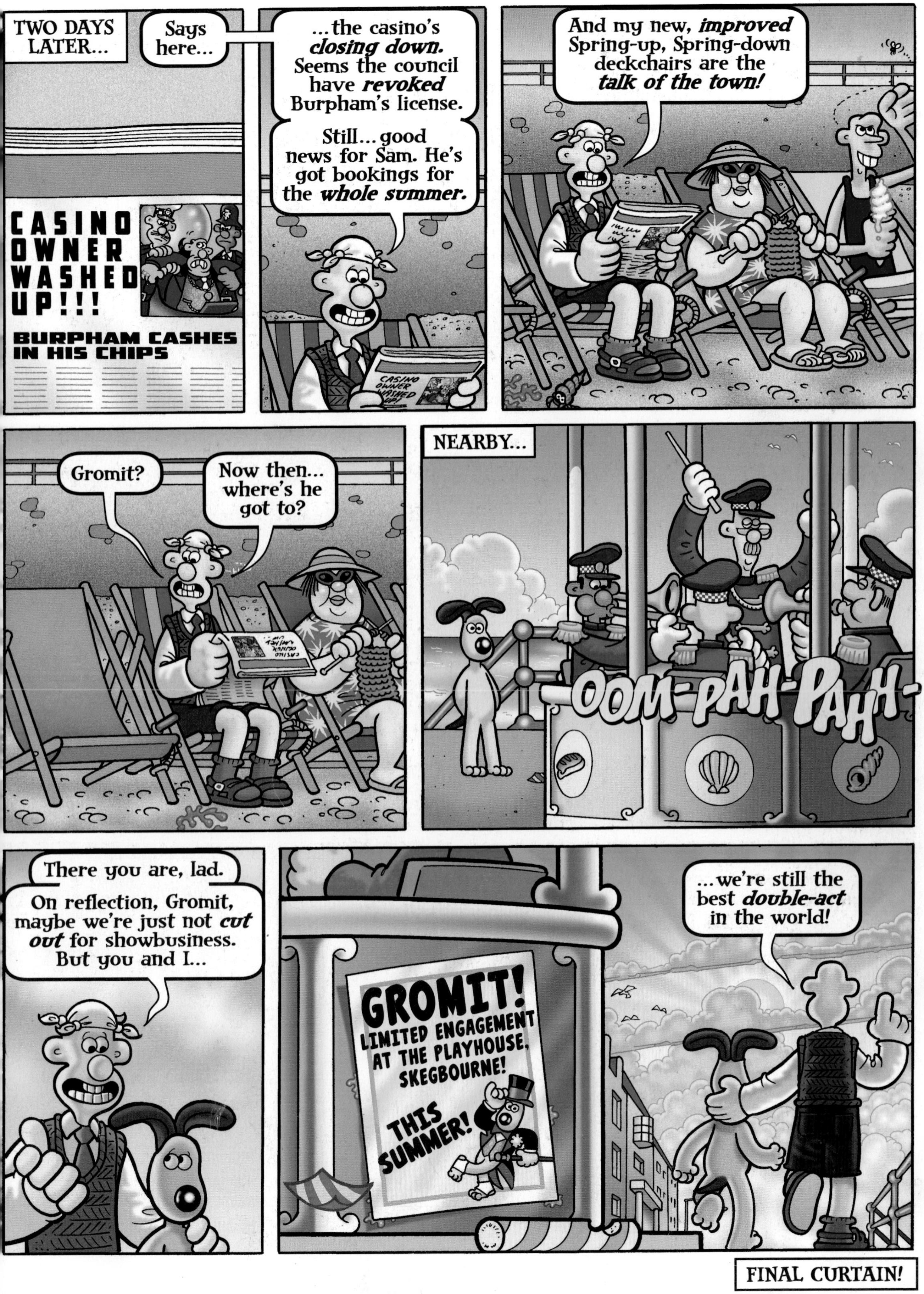

TWO DAYS LATER...
Says here...
...the casino's *closing down.* Seems the council have *revoked* Burpham's license.
Still... good news for Sam. He's got bookings for the *whole summer.*
CASINO OWNER WASHED UP!!!
BURPHAM CASHES IN HIS CHIPS
CASINO OWNER WASHED UP!
And my new, *improved* Spring-up, Spring-down deckchairs are the *talk of the town!*
Gromit?
Now then... where's he got to?
NEARBY...
OOM-PAH-PAHH-
There you are, lad.
On reflection, Gromit, maybe we're just not *cut out* for showbusiness. But you and I...
GROMIT! LIMITED ENGAGEMENT AT THE PLAYHOUSE, SKEGBOURNE! THIS SUMMER!
...we're still the best *double-act* in the world!
FINAL CURTAIN!

CHECK OUT THESE OTHER CRACKING COLLECTIONS FROM TITAN BOOKS!

Aardman
presents
Wallace & Gromit
Catch of the Day

Wallace & Gromit:
Catch of the Day

Aardman
presents
Wallace & Gromit
The Whippet Vanishes

Wallace & Gromit:
The Whippet Vanishes

Aardman
presents
Wallace & Gromit
The Bootiful Game

Wallace & Gromit:
The Bootiful Game

FANTASTIC FREE PENCIL CASE!
1ST ISSUE
Aardman
Wallace & Gromit
Comic
EPIC ADVENTURES!
AWESOME INVENTIONS!
No.1 Oct 2005 £2.50

Wallace & Gromit: The Comic!
Available at all good newsagents

www.titanbooks.com

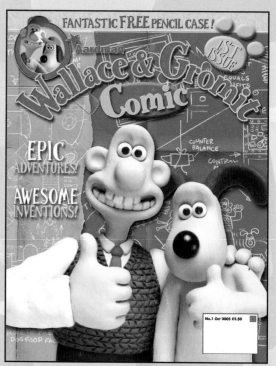